MOODY PRESS
CHICAGO

© 1994 by
MIRIAM BUNDY

All rights reserved. No part of this book may be reproduced in any form without permission in writing from the publisher, except in the case of brief quotations embodied in critical articles or reviews.

All Scripture quotations, unless indicated, are taken from the *Holy Bible: New International Version*®. NIV®. Copyright © 1973, 1978, 1984, International Bible Society. Used by permission of Zondervan Publishing House. All rights reserved.

The use of selected references from various versions of the Bible in this publication does not necessarily imply publisher endorsement of the versions in their entirety.

ISBN: 0-8024-2736-7

1 3 5 7 9 10 8 6 4 2

Printed in the United States of America

Contents

Preface	7
1. Women on the Edge: Watching the Celebration	9

PART ONE: COMMITMENT POWER

2. A Choice of Mind	21
3. A Choice of Honor	31
4. A Choice of Heart	47
5. A Choice of Triumph	63

PART TWO: COMMUNICATION POWER

6. Communications that Promote Communion	75
7. Communications that Encourage Trust	85
8. Communications that Build Dreams	95
9. Communications that Face Conflict	107

PART THREE: CONFIRMATION POWER

10. Confirming Purpose in the Home	127
11. Confirming Intentions in Leadership	143
12. Confirming Worth in the Workplace	153
13. Confirming Opportunities as Friends	163
14. Confirming Authenticity in Diverse Communities	179

STUDY GUIDE

Women in the Center: Sharing the Celebration	191

Preface

Softly she pleaded, "What would you do?"

She was a woman caught in the crevice between fear and anger, surprised by gender discrimination and both stimulated and shocked by the secular and religious debate about women. She wondered if something strange were happening to her.

She wanted to know what reason I would have for hope in her circumstances. She interpreted the instruction for suffering women to put their hope in God as insensitive and simplistic, though I knew it to be a complex and realistic process. I began to dig deeper, listening, reading the wide range of secular and religious feminist literature, and searching the Scriptures. Were the words of God, especially phrases such as "be submissive," and "rejoice in suffering," unfair and irrelevant to women walking into the twenty-first century?

Within the pages of the Bible I rediscovered three dynamic reasons for women to hope. Every woman can find peace and empowerment to celebrate the feminine mission by following the biblical principles of commitment, communication, and confirmation. These principles will work in your life even if you don't know that they came from the Bible.

The whisper of that woman's question still echoes in my ears. It presses me to write and encourage you to search the Scriptures. Alone or with a group open your heart and mind to listen, study, and discuss what you would do.

The Celebration of Womanhood

"Always be prepared to give an answer to everyone who asks you to give the reason for the hope that you have. But do this with gentleness and respect" (1 Peter 3:15).

1

Women on the Edge: Watching the Celebration

We were startled and laughed.

The loudspeaker boomed in the Anaheim stadium, "USC, number eighty, penalty for excessive celebration." What was that?

Johnnie Morton, the great runner and wide receiver for the University of Southern California, had just made a touchdown, rolled on the grass and, with obvious glee, kicked his heels. The officials called it excessive celebration.

Yes, we laughed. It was an unexpected call, a new rule for the 1993 football season. How can one measure celebration? Isn't that the fun of football—celebration?

A few weeks later another referee called the same penalty at the San Bernardino Valley College opening football game. That time the player was obviously taunting the other team, daringly holding the football out to his pursuer as he ran into the end zone.

It made me think about the meaning of celebration. At a sports event, the fans are celebrating more than a singular moment of excitement. We rejoice because we vicariously put ourselves on the line with the players, cheering, moaning, grunting, supporting their teamwork and self-discipline, their sheer guts to get up and go when knocked and blocked— their ability to go through the process to reach that winning moment. Celebration commemorates action.

The Celebration of Womanhood

We have birthday parties, anniversary dinners, wedding ceremonies, grand openings. Celebration commemorates a happening.

There are happy celebrations and sad celebrations, solemn celebrations and mocking celebrations. A woman in California helps people celebrate their divorce with ceremonial vows to "have and to hold anyone I choose," concluding with the woman smashing her wedding ring with a sledgehammer. Her business, which includes the service of redesigning the jewelry (the stone is removed before the smash), is called "Ring of Freedom." That's excessive celebration.

"Ring of Freedom" celebrates a lack of life with destructive action. In contrast, the "Feminine Mission" celebrates a fullness in life with constructive action.

Getting a Life

In the yearning for action in life, as in sports, more and more women are coming out of the stands and coming down to the field, asking to be active participants. Both in the stands and on the field voices of cheering and cursing are causing tension, great confusion, and little celebration for women.

Some voices still insist that a woman should not play, but she should just watch and support. Others call out, "Go for it! Get down on the field." And some say, "Just sit over here and keep score."

We are urged to probe our feminine spirit.
To protest the roles of womanhood.
To seek our worth.
To save ourselves.
Is this celebration?
We are told to surrender.
Exist for man.

Just function.
Do not question.
Is this celebration?
Shouting with joy to God.
Singing with glory to His name.
Saying to God, "How awesome are your deeds!"
This sounds like celebration.
But how does a woman rejoice in the day that the Lord has made
when she is pushed and pulled,
then left on the edge by those who revere and demean?

Solutions come from every side. The feminists, pop feminists, postfeminists, egalitarians, traditionalists, biblical feminists, Christian feminists, and evangelical egalitarians are all eager to coach the women of the world. "Come play on my team, and you'll have something to celebrate," they call.

The great draw of the coach is the position she offers other women. "Well, I'm really just a stay-at-home kind of woman, so I'll play on the traditionalist team," says one.

"I like the role supported by the egalitarians," says another.

Identifying the Teams

The Religious League

Hierarchical Traditionalist. This team celebrates creation order, the equal worth of the sexes, roles, or submission in ministry and marriage, and it claims the inerrancy and authority of the Scriptures.

Evangelical Egalitarian/Biblical Feminist. This team celebrates equal rights and roles of sexes in ministry and marriage and claims inerrancy and authority of the Scriptures.

Christian Feminist. This team celebrates women's rights and claims a Christian worldview.

The Celebration of Womanhood

Feminists for Life. This team celebrates equal rights and pro-life values, based on religious convictions.

The Secular League

Radical Feminist. This team celebrates a woman's right to dominate or disregard men, condemns patriarchy, and claims a humanistic worldview.

Pop Feminist. This team celebrates women's rights while applauding chivalry and androgyny and claims a humanistic worldview.

Postfeminist. This team celebrates equal rights for men, the understanding of androgynous humanity, and the discovery of the feminine spirit in man, and it claims a humanistic worldview.

Egalitarian. This team celebrates the equal rights and roles of sexes and claims a humanistic worldview.

Debating Place

The great debate between authors, educators, theologians, and ordinary people like you and me is about the issue of a woman's place. Many women feel as if they are merely observers of the celebration—on the edge looking in. The voices of experts shout confidently and whisper seductively. Their words are effective. The nineties is the decade for women. Loud victory speeches pronounce the glories of equality in the game.

But wait. The celebration is dying down. There is a hush. Now everyone entering the field must wear a badge. Each one shows the label of his or her persuasion. Those who are unsure are assigned to the bench of the "uncommitted." The competition on the field is accelerating. Feminists and traditionalists of all descriptions are blocking and tackling each other—feminists opposing traditionalists, hierarchalists opposing evangelical egalitarians. It looks like a fight. And millions of people who are slugging their fists are not even sure what it's about.

Calling Time Out

Let's take a little time out to dream. Imagine women of all ages, from all times, and of all colors and cultures are freely, confidently, and compassionately moving across the playing field, unaware of the power of blessing that lingers in their path. Like a pungent sweet aroma, they energize actions that give us cause for pure celebration.

In reality, strong and gentle women, soft women, hearty women, determined women, and contented women, each with unique talents and personalities, interact with harmony, permeating the atmosphere with beauty, giving fullness to life. *What is their secret?* we wonder.

Before we can ask, the whistle blows and the game begins again. But something is wrong. It looks like it is every player for him- or herself. The teams are divided. They have lost their power. The fans are leaving. Now some players are dropping out. I catch up with one player as she reaches the gate.

"Excuse me," I call as the young woman turns and stares. The look on her face is so bland that I am momentarily stuck for a question. "What's the matter?" I blurt. "Why are you leaving?"

"Isn't it obvious?" she asks with disdain.

"Obvious?"

"Yeah. I know this game as well as any man on the field. And I was proud of my position on the team. I thought, at last, I could be who I was meant to be."

"Of course," I try to encourage her with a confidential tone. "Then why . . . ?"

"Don't you know?" Her question is shaming. "Don't you know? Didn't you see the craziness out there? There was no way we could accomplish our mission. I thought my position was the key. But the team never connected. We had no power. It was no fun, so I quit!"

She leaves the field and disappears.

I am stunned. I had read about her struggle for a position on the team. It was a cause célèbre. She had been so joyous, and now suddenly she was out of the game. There was nothing to celebrate. She had finally reached the place where she wanted to be, but she lacked the power to complete her mission.

Assigned to Watch

Power is the primary issue in a discussion of gender discrimination. Every woman of every age and culture at some time, to some degree experiences the feeling of powerlessness. Consider:

The Complaint	*The Question*	*The Issue*
Abuse	Are we human?	Power to live in peace
Career limitations	Are we equal?	Power to choose
Discrimination against singles	Are we worthy?	Power to be free
Women's choices considered last	Are we equal?	Power to be fulfilled
Role determines value	Are we recognized?	Power to be individuals
Ministry limits	Are we redeemed?	Power to use gifts

The majority of the literature and discussion about gender issues focuses on a woman's role or place, and it is not satisfying women's real needs or answering their frustrations. The problem is "place" only in the sense that women feel as if they are often watching the celebration of life when they really wish to be an active part of it.

Must a woman be dependent on a man? Must she submit, support, and be silent in his presence? Must she wait on the edge, watching the celebration?

Woman was created by God for a unique, feminine mission: to create communion, to inspire vision and hope, to do right without fear, to affirm and sustain life, to reflect glory. To actively enter into the celebration of life she must identify her personal mission as a woman and commit not only her mind but her behavior to the fulfillment of that mission. Every woman can experience the power to celebrate, communicate, and confirm the value of womanhood everyday as she commits to the feminine mission.

The purpose of this book is to help you understand what the feminine mission is and how you can discover the joy and power of celebrating that mission.

Encouraged to Join

Throughout this book questions and exercises will be included to help you personalize the information to fit your needs and desires. As you join the process of discovering your personal mission, you will find that though some of the subjects are complex, you will be able to choose how gradually or quickly you want to integrate the suggested activities into your daily life. Some readers will want to concentrate on one activity more than another. Others may wish to devour and digest the whole volume.

To understand the approach of this book, let us look at a "replay" of an incident between two women in the New Testament who were arguing over the issue of their mission. We are not shown the details, but our picture reports the response of "coach" Paul. He was out of town at the time of the big fight between Euodia and Syntyche, but he definitely heard about it. It was all over the news. So he sent word back to the team: "Help these women learn to

The Celebration of Womanhood

celebrate!" (His words: "Rejoice in the Lord always. I will say it again: Rejoice!" [Philippians 4:4]).

Paul does not say that they can't express their true feelings, but he urges them not to be so sharp and intense. "Let your gentleness be evident to all. . . . Do not be anxious" (4:5–6).

Compare that with another replay, and you will begin to see the direction of our study. Coach Peter noticed the frustration of some women who were so eager to accept the idea of celebration that they forgot the meaning of their mission. Our picture shows Peter explaining the problem to those women:

"It's not your jewels and the clothes that create a celebration," he says. "You cannot force someone else to celebrate no matter how enthusiastically you may talk. Focus on your mission!" Then he adds, "If you really want to celebrate (literally, to love life and see good days), you must understand the principles of commitment power (turn from evil and do good), communication power (keep your tongue from evil and lips from deceitful speech), and confirmation power (seek peace and pursue it)" (see 1 Peter 3).

In this book you will be encouraged to study biblical models of the feminine mission and to define your personal mission as a woman. Then, as we investigate the practical meaning of the three empowerment principles, you will have the opportunity to see how they apply to your life through questions, exercises, and the option of research. This approach does not propose a Polyannaish ignorance of abuse, evil, and discrimination; rather, it faces the reality of what a woman can do in difficult circumstances.

In the first section, we will look at the power of commitment in our mission. What do I mean by "commitment"? Is submission good or bad? How do we determine our mission? How do we answer the arguments of others? Both theological and secular sources will be considered in this process. We will see what commitment power is: a choice of mind, a choice of honor, a choice of heart, and a choice of triumph.

Part 2 explains the power of communication in our mission. How can we change our circumstances? Should we be angry? What can a woman do? We will see that communication power creates hope as we listen to, love, speak to, and confront others.

The power of confirmation in our mission will be our third main area of consideration. Though we will tackle some of the tough questions, I do not intend to tell you your place. You will have the opportunity to develop mission guidelines for your particular situation through a progressive personal study. You will find the principles, process, and practical examples of choices and consequences.

Whereas other works stress the importance of a woman's place and the once-for-all resolution of issues, *The Celebration of Womanhood* stresses the greater importance of the process of commitment to daily conduct that is consistent with a godly mission. My desire is to help you step into your dream, applying the reality of your eternal purpose to life situations. You can share in the celebration—firsthand. It's your choice.

Discovering Your Mission

1. What is the position of women in your cultural setting? Are the roles desired or predetermined?
2. How have you personally experienced limitation of power as a woman? Why do you think that is?

Further Research

Read the book of 1 Peter in the New Testament. As you read, substitute the word discrimination for the word suffering. Then note the following: Who is discriminated against? How? Why? What does it mean to be discriminated against?

Part One

COMMITMENT POWER

The Principle of Commitment Power

As the dynamic action of commitment integrates your energies, intellect, and will, you will be empowered to celebrate the feminine mission.

The Models of Commitment Power

Sarah, the wife of Abraham, shows us how commitment power enabled her to survive abuse and disappointment while demonstrating serenity.

Ruth, the widowed daughter-in-law of Naomi, illustrates how a single woman can celebrate the feminine mission, despite grief and loss.

Esther reveals how commitment power leads us to the secret of triumph in the feminine mission.

2

A Choice of Mind

*It is not good to have zeal without knowledge,
nor to be hasty and miss the way.*

Proverbs 19:2

It seemed impossible that someone I knew, that sparkling teenager who baby-sat our children, who shared reports of her good times and goals with us as we drove her home, had been knocked down the stairs by her husband.

"Anna? Not Anna," I objected to her mother.

"She has a broken rib," her mother reported despondently. "She's hiding from him. She's afraid he'll hurt the children."

I pictured Anna, the giving, loving teenager whom we watched grow into a beautiful young woman. She dreamed of a career—maybe pediatric nursing, she said. Then she met a handsome man and submitted all her dreams to him. He was a few years older than she was, and he offered her a home and a family of her own. She finished high school, started a job, and was married.

"This has happened before," her mother continued.

Anna's husband had always appeared likable and loving in our presence. Mike and Anna? I was heartsick. She had been one of my best baby-sitters, bathing, feeding, and cleaning up after the children while managing to entertain them. She was strong enough to handle my three spirited children while genuinely caring for them. She was not weak. How could it happen?

What had happened to Anna? Gifted, gracious, and a God-fearing young woman, she relinquished her identity and intelligence to the man she loved. She was a woman on the edge. Could she have avoided such unhappiness, or was she a victim of a wanton world system? And who was Mike, really?

He was in his twenties, with one shattered marriage already behind him but intent on caring for the new woman in his life. Anna interpreted his dominance as manliness. She told me she was eager to marry and, with barely a pause, excused the failure of his first marriage. Mike vowed to follow God in his life, pledging allegiance to the same faith as Anna. She was confident they would make a fresh start. As Mike's abusive behavior began to surface, Anna dutifully submitted, as she believed her faith taught her, until the fateful fall down the stairs. Then fear forced her to flee. Did Mike really think he was following God's plan for the marriage relationship, asserting control as head? Did Anna continue to excuse Mike's behavior out of respectful observance of her vows of obedience?

Anna made a choice that severely complicated her world. Though she did not willingly become a victim of physical and mental abuse, for some time she repeatedly accepted degrading episodes because she was not clear about her mission as a woman.

Women who make choices without knowledge of their mission are women on the edge.

What Is a Mission?

You may have friends like Anna. You may work with them, worship with them, or live in the same neighborhood. Watch and listen. Perhaps they have hidden their hurts and their confusion, hesitant to tell you of the pain of an experience or of a continuing circumstance of inequitable treatment.

A Choice of Mind

What happens when we make certain choices—some more voluntary than others—that push us to the edge, making us feel trapped, left without options, and misunderstood? We become like a player on the athletic field who has no power—alone, perhaps angry, unfulfilled, and searching for another place to be.

Our minds crave a clear understanding of our direction or purpose. That is what we define as mission: a purpose.

Does your mission purpose look like

- an enlarged "To Do" list?
- a game plan for success?
- a practice schedule of talent development?
- a water girl's diary?

Do you believe you were created as a woman for a special purpose? Have you thought about your mission, or do you pray just to survive the urgencies of the day?

Perhaps you have considered this question and think in terms of your "calling" in life. But your "call" may or may not relate to your mission. Consider the calls that are confused with purpose when we are not sure about our mission.

The Call to Care

Sometimes in marriage we become caretakers of parents or children, as the result of illness or in our work. If we give and give, believing that giving is our mission, we often give out. We're pushed to the edge. Without the knowledge and understanding of a deeper purpose we look for gratitude from the recipients as our reward. When it is not expressed it is easy to become resentful and disillusioned about our purpose.

The Celebration of Womanhood

The Call to Perform

If we believe that a woman's purpose is to serve, what happens when we cannot perform? If we are physically, emotionally, or financially dependent on others, have we lost our purpose?

The Call to Become

Authors such as Raine Eisler grasp the imagination of readers with alluring vocabulary, urging us to become androgynous forms of humanity or to find a new feminine self. Though the idea of becoming in touch with our inner selves, our feminine selves, or our former selves is not a new proposal, it has found a resurgence in the new age and feminist movements. The zeal of the women in those movements is undeniable. However, if you follow zeal without knowledge—no matter how in touch you may feel with yourself—you will lose touch with the world around you; thus, the proposal becomes purposeless.

The Call to Relate

At one point the meaning of Anna's life was dependent on her relationship to Mike. As he abused her love, her life became not only less meaningful but miserable. If you measure your worth and purpose by your relationships, you will find yourself on the edge. As a friend you may not always be needed; as a lover you may not always be desired; as a mentor or mother you may not always be appreciated. Though our mission affects our relationships, the act of relating is not our mission.

A mission statement defines the reason for our being and the ultimate purpose of our activity. Churches and institutions of business write mission statements to make their reason for being and purpose of activity clear to everyone. It becomes the guideline for decisions, answering questions such as: Should we undertake this activity? Is it compatible with our mission?

Our mission, then, is a goal larger than caring, performing, becoming, or relating. First, we must decide what we believe about the creation of women and ask, "For what purpose was the first woman formed?" Then we must ask how that relates to the reason of our lives—to our personal purpose as individual women. It is the basis of your worldview, not your reactions to world problems—however noble they may be—that gives meaning to your mission.

What Choices Do Women Have?

An awareness of the wide spectrum of directions in which some women search for solutions to their problems can help us understand the importance of thoughtfully determining our mission. Consider some of the earnest choices women have made and where they lead.

The Choice to Express Bitterness

The small group meetings were intimate and friendly, encouraging the participants to share their feelings. The leader guided the discussion and challenged the group to rethink their views. A small group Bible study? No. It was the format for Mao Tse-tung's "speaking bitterness" groups in the 1940s. Women were encouraged to verbalize their agony and hatred of war crimes. As they met, instead of feeling repressed, they found strength and resolve to act against their perpetrators.[1]

Whereas the long history of the feminist movement reveals both good and bad agendas, the most radical aberrations are motivated by anger and supported by those who refute the Judeo-Christian paradigm. Unfortunately many extremists who harbor bitterness lose the power to celebrate life.

The Choice to Separate

Some women have decided that the solution to injustice is segregation. Such women urge, "Let us separate our learning, our language, our leadership, and our leisure."

Separate learning. Women's studies, or gender role studies, have been popularized throughout the Western world for the past twenty years. Though attention to specialized information is good, the joy of discovery and learning is often diminished by those who are intent upon indoctrination. Professor Joyce Treblicot of Washington University in St. Louis "readily admits that her mission is to indoctrinate students."[2]

She states that the goal of her "ovulars" (her word to replace the "sexist" term "seminar") is to convert others to her "dyke" philosophy. A symbol of her separation is the substitution of the word "wimmin" for "women" in an effort to completely individualize the female name.

Separate language. Many women (and men) consider biblical language patriarchal and, therefore, offensive. Thus new translations of Scripture change the traditional words for the Trinity from Father, Son, and Holy Spirit to Creator, Redeemer, and Sustainer, or Source, Servant, and Guide to more accurately reflect the "androgynous" nature of God.

Separate leadership. Some of the leadership as well, within both the traditional and feminist movements, reveals separate agendas. Some traditionalists, under the guise of women's movements, are in actuality leading a political or wealth crusade, and some feminists use the platform of equality to champion lesbianism and witchery. Just as we must be careful not to assume that all traditionalists or feminists are pushing hidden agendas, we must be discerning about the message that is communicated by our alignment with self-serving or reactionary leadership.

Separate leisure. It has also become more common in Europe and the United States for some women to refuse to have any contact with men at all—not in their work or social life, and even eating exclusively in restaurants where men are not permitted at any time.[3]

The Choice to Cocoon

One extreme reaction to the confusing subject of the needs and rights of women is to avoid the issue altogether. Even a thoughtful consideration of our culture and the needs of women today is viewed as unacceptable. Out of fear, some women build a safe cocoon of comfortable information around them. They are not bothered by or moved to end injustice because they are completely insulated from it.

The Choice to Retreat

What about the women who do recognize in others and in themselves the experience of Anna? They continue to seek spiritual answers, turning back to their roots. But what happens to those whose pleas go unheard? I see them shifting to another extreme edge, turning away from biblical truth to focus solely on women's movements, cultic wisdom that anesthetizes their pain, or an absorbing career that becomes a substitute for the resolution of problems.

When we allow reactions of retreat and revenge to determine our purpose, even good endeavors can bind our minds and push us to the edge.

Who Are the Women on the Edge?

There are women on the edge all around us, seeking ancient secrets. They are women of all ages, from all circumstances, who are unable to celebrate the feminine mission. In one way or another they feel left out, pushed aside

The Celebration of Womanhood

without any means of controlling the events of their lives. Are they really struggling with genderless issues, personal issues regarding peace and power? Are they simply victims of dysfunctional relationships? Or do they grapple with the mystery of the feminine mission?

Particularly in the church, the constant tension about women's issues continues to hurt rather than heal. Our souls are saturated with theories and theology about equality, empowerment, and the roles of women. What difference does it make what we believe about how and why we were created?

Though the theology of women's issues becomes more complex in each new cultural and communication setting, there is great purpose and value in womanhood. Just as the rising sun gives us new light each morning to see the beauty of creation, our daily recognition of the reason for our creation will shine new light on the grace and glory of the feminine mission. The feminine mission is a choice of the mind. The first step toward celebrating your mission is to make a choice to seek knowledge and understanding of its meaning.

What you believe about your mission—why you were created woman—can make the difference between secondhand or personal celebration. Are you willing to investigate the facts, to consider the authority of the Creator of the universe?

"If you accept my words and store up my commands within you, turning your ear to wisdom and applying your heart to understanding, . . . then you will understand the fear of the Lord and find the knowledge of God" (Proverbs 2:1–2, 5). You can discover a reason to celebrate! It's a choice of the mind.

Discovering Your Mission

1. List three everyday activities that you are called to do. Do you see ways in which you tend to measure the value of your existence by your success or failure in those activities? How?
2. When you begin a new day how is your purpose for that day affected by your ability to perform, to become or discover a new self, or by the success or failure of relationships?
3. Do you sometimes feel like a woman on the edge? Why?
4. Examine your initial reaction to the choices to express bitterness, to separate, to cocoon, to retreat. Do you sometimes exhibit one of those reactions? How does the realization of this identity affect your behavior and perception of yourself?

Further Research

1. Select a group that is connected with women's issues and find their mission statement. If possible determine the basis for their statement.
2. Three books that describe differing viewpoints on this issue are: *Beyond Power: On Women, Men, and Morals*, by Marilyn French; *The Feminist Gospel*, by Mary Kassian; and *Daughters of the Church*, by Ruth Tucker. Compare the personal biographies of those authors. Why do you think they developed such different viewpoints?

NOTES

1. Mary A. Kassian, *The Feminist Gospel* (Wheaton, Ill.: Crossway, 1992), 61.
2. "Seminars Are Out; 'Ovulars' Are In," *Campus Alert* 1, no. 3 (September 1993), 4.
3. Marilyn French, *Beyond Power: On Women, Men, and Morals* (New York: Summit, 1985), 447.

3

A Choice of Honor

Your beauty . . . should be that of your inner self. . . .
This is the way the holy women of the past . . .
used to make themselves beautiful.

1 Peter 3:3–5

A unique organization called The Daughters of Sarah uses the historical image of the biblical Sarah as a metaphor for many feminist causes, including lesbianism.[1] Biblical history confirms the significance of Sarah; however, it contradicts the approach of The Daughters of Sarah.

First Peter 3:6 states that we are daughters of Sarah if we "do what is right and do not give way to fear." That Scripture is used as the basis for The Daughters of Sarah's tie to the historical figure of Sarah. Can you see the error in using Sarah's struggles as the basis of forming this feminist group?

The inaccurate application of the image of Sarah is furthered when individual emotions and experiences are isolated from the whole of history. If we are to make a choice of honor in the acceptance of our mission, we must begin with an honest investigation of the truth of Scripture. When feelings cloud our reasoning our tendency is to measure the truth against our feelings, rather than first seeking to examine what is truth.

Historically and scripturally, Sarah is cited as a model for women. Therefore, we will begin our pursuit of understanding the feminine mission by examining her life and comparing it with some reflections about Eve, the first woman God created.

Four interpersonal relationships will form the basis for our study: the relationships of Sarah and Eve as they reveal the source of the feminine mission; the relationship of Sarah to Abraham as it exposes the secret of the feminine mission; the relationship of Sarah to God as it shows the spirit of the feminine mission; and the relationship of Sarah to us as it multiplies the sharing of the feminine mission.

The Source of the Feminine Mission

A decade ago, I took a new look at the book of 1 Peter, noting that the few words written about Sarah beyond her biography in Genesis make specific reference to her beauty and her behavior.

As often as we are impressed in Scripture with the necessity of inner beauty, more than once the outward beauty of a woman is extolled. Kings of sophisticated populations were so attracted by Sarah that she won their hearts without a contest. Even beyond the age of sixty she was sought out by Abimelech. It was a practice of powerful men of that time to acquire on sight the women they fancied. One must assume that Sarah was a stunning beauty.

What was so magnetic about Sarah that at sixty she was still preferred to younger women? Sarah knew a secret about the feminine mission that began with Eve long ago. Her secret not only helped her maintain an irresistible quality within but, I believe, enhanced her physical beauty as well.

Eve was undoubtedly a beauty herself as God's first model of womanhood. She was uniquely created, not as a second man, a duplicate Adam, or a brother, but as a woman especially created to fulfill a mission that another man could not. Although of equal worth and value as the man Adam, the woman Eve was not identical to him. She was a fully human individual and a perfect match for him.

A Choice of Honor

In the creation of Eve we see the first clue to the purpose of woman: she was distinctive from man, yet she was of equal dignity and worth. So what was her mission?

With Adam she was to rule and subdue the earth, to be fruitful and multiply. Some may argue that at the time of the Fall and the Curse woman was devalued, that she became less worthy and her mission changed. Though certainly the conditions of her life changed, her mission remained the same.

What happened to Eve? She must have felt great remorse when she saw the results of her actions. She not only lost her innocence, she brought shame to her husband. Her secure and serene world vanished. For the first time she knew fear.

How could she go on? If she gave in to fear and anxiety could she continue to be the "life-giver" her name implies? Though we know little of Eve's actions or communications after the Garden, her responses to the births of Cain and Seth are noteworthy: "With the help of the Lord I have brought forth a man" (Genesis 4:1), and, "God has granted me another child in place of Abel" (4:25). Eve learned to put her hope in God and not give in to fear.

Peter says the same thing about Sarah: "For this is the way the holy women of the past who put their hope in God used to make themselves beautiful. They were submissive to their own husbands, like Sarah, who obeyed Abraham and called him her master. You are her daughters if you do what is right and do not give way to fear" (1 Peter 3:5–6).

Though the consequences of our sins and circumstances may make the going tough, they do not disqualify us from pursuing the feminine mission. Just as Eve learned to put her hope in God, we, too, can trust God as the originator and the source of our mission.

The Celebration of Womanhood

The Secret of the Feminine Mission

The secret of the feminine mission is exposed in Sarah's relationship to Abraham as recorded in Genesis 11–23. Although she was a beautiful woman, married to a wealthy man, Sarah experienced many troubles. She knew the heartache of longing for a child. She knew the trauma of moving and adapting to foreign lands. She knew the grief of losing a family member to unthinkable circumstances (Lot's wife). She knew the pain of being humiliated by her maid, who produced a child for her husband when she had failed. She was twice asked by her husband to deny their relationship as husband and wife and subsequently taken into the households of strange men. Any one of those circumstances could have destroyed her relationship with Abraham.

What do we see in Sarah's response that reveals the secret of the feminine mission?

Sarah's words are not included in the early narrative, but we can glean insight from her actions. Sarah moved not only away from her homeland to Haran but to Ur and then to Canaan and Egypt. When her husband feared acceptance in a new place, she went far beyond what any woman would consider today and pretended that she was only his sister. It was true that Terah was the father of both Abraham and Sarah, but they were born of different mothers. I don't know how a husband could make such a request of his wife, considering the potential consequences, but Sarah agreed. She took into account the reason behind his request, and she loved him unselfishly, sacrificing her own comfort for the sake of his life. Her actions were characterized by submission and trust.

What about her words? The first words of Sarah recorded for us appear in Genesis 16. God had promised to give Abraham children, to make him the father of a great nation, but Sarah was unable to have a child. Maybe God meant to fulfill His promise without her, she thought. In the ancient Hebrew culture it was not uncommon for a man to have more than one wife. If Sarah couldn't have her own child, maybe she could arrange for a surrogate mother. "Perhaps I can build a family through her" (16:2).

He agreed. So she gave her maid, Hagar, to Abraham as his wife. Unfortunately, it came to be a decision that she regretted. Hagar despised her mistress when she realized she was to have a child and Sarah could not. Abraham's childless state was Sarah's fault.

Sarah was obviously distressed, but instead of letting bitterness take root and grow, she confronted her husband honestly with her feelings. Was it wrong to be upset with Abraham when the suggestion to marry Hagar had first come from her? Perhaps. But her honest, open expression shifted the responsibility for a decision to his shoulders. Little else is revealed about Sarah's conversations with Abraham but that she was obedient and respectful, calling him her master.

From our sketch of Sarah and her relationship with Abraham we observe two behaviors:

1. She related respectfully to her husband in words and actions, listening to his requests and loving him with commitment to his best.
2. She recognized his responsibility in their relationship, releasing accountability for decisions to him, confronting him honestly, overcoming the temptation to circumvent his authority.

A study of Sarah's life does not reveal meekness and mildness. She withstood many hardships and was capable of a harsh response, as in the case of Hagar. Although she carried the strength of her personality into her marriage, she did not fight God's plan for the direction of her life but allowed it to fortify her relationship with Abraham.

The Spirit of the Feminine Mission

Scripture provides three brief outlines of Sarah's reflections on God. The spirit of the feminine mission is revealed in these accounts.

When she learns that she is promised a baby, Sarah, who had longed for a child for many decades, laughs with amusement, saying she is now "worn out." When confronted, however, she quickly denies her doubt.

The very next scene in which Sarah appears reveals the birth of her son and reflects the joy of her communication of praise: "God has brought me laughter, and everyone who hears about this will laugh with me. Who would have said to Abraham that Sarah would nurse children? Yet I have borne him a son in his old age" (Genesis 21:7).

Have you ever hoped and longed for a child? Our daughter Grace brought such delight to us from the moment of her birth that when she began to walk, we thought it would be wonderful to have another child. Our hopes were raised and crushed twice when two babies miscarried. Then God sent us a precious little son, Jonathan, through the process of adoption. Then another pregnancy ended. Each one was wrenchingly difficult, a loss only understood through experience.

I can imagine Sarah's doubt. After tears, we steel ourselves. But a tender wound is always touched by the birth of a new baby. Sarah could have argued, "I have reason to laugh," but she quickly realized her mistake and reverenced the words spoken to her. She was wrong to deny her doubt and lie. But she was right to respect God's authority.

Sarah might have complained that at her age she didn't need the pain of childbirth; after all, she had accepted her state. But she submitted to the timing of God's plan with joy. I know about that joy of the unexpected too. Another treasured girl was born to us, and we named her Valerie.

In 1 Peter, our last glimpse of Sarah is captioned with the notation for us to seek to be like her. The secret of her beauty was on the inside. She followed God's plan in her relationship to her husband, and she put her hope in God.

The record of Sarah's encounters with God show us that positive interpersonal relationships are characterized by (1) a responsible spirit, seeking to support, trust, and follow the one in authority, and (2) an open spirit, respectfully expressing honest emotions.

Sarah shows us that a woman has a unique opportunity to influence relationships in the direction of positive, productive, and peaceful development.

The Sharing of the Feminine Mission

The relationship of Sarah to us multiplies the sharing of the feminine mission.

Many women of the past put their hope in God, making themselves beautiful by submitting to their husbands. But Sarah is chosen as the model for this principle. The Scripture says we are her daughters if we "do what is right and do not give way to fear."

Imagine the women of Sarah's time. They must have wondered, "What is her secret? She is so beautiful." We are not told how she responded to other women. But we do know that "holy women of the past" followed her model. Perhaps she shared her secrets. She was without children for most of her years, so I'd like to think she mentored others.

The Celebration of Womanhood

Clues to the Feminine Mission

Our sketches have revealed much about the feminine mission. We saw in the drawings of Sarah and Eve that God is the source of the feminine mission; in later glimpses of Sarah with Abraham we learned the secret of their relationship (and the secret of a successful mission) summarized in two words: respect and responsibility; in the portrait of Sarah's response to God we learned the importance of a spirit of openness and responsibility; and in Sarah's example as a model for others we saw that her sensitive submission to and honor of Abraham was related to the feminine mission.

Now What?

We have seen that the first step to understanding the feminine mission is to seek knowledge. That is a choice of the mind. It is not difficult to agree that the pursuit of knowledge is good. But the heady allure of this step often imprisons us in the world of academia. We must free ourselves from endless rhetorical debate and step into the reality of life by choosing to define our purpose as it relates to authority and truth as opposed to experience and emotion. In this book we accept the premise that "the word of God is living and active. Sharper than any double-edged sword, it penetrates even to dividing soul and spirit, joints and marrow; it judges the thoughts and attitudes of the heart" (Hebrews 4:12). From this Word, the Bible, we will seek to understand the feminine mission.

What then do the examples of Eve and Sarah suggest? Are men inseparable from the meaning of our mission? Have single women been overlooked? Clearly, the whole of Scripture shows that the feminine mission extends far beyond the bonds of marriage. Every woman in every circumstance can choose to celebrate her life. Rather than being excluded because your experience is different, you are given a choice to be included because the historical, authoritative foundation for the feminine mission is the same for every woman. To follow the feminine mission does not mean risking your life for a place of uncertainty. It involves putting your hope in a Person of security. It is not an ignominious choice. It is a choice of honor.

Discovering Your Mission

1. Can you identify instances in your life when your emotions have clouded your understanding of truth?
2. Choose a women's issue, and determine how you think Sarah would have responded with reference to:
   Expression of feelings
   Response to injustice
   Source of authority
   Perception of mission
3. How did Eve differ from Adam in her behavior?
4. What do you think was the secret of Sarah's beauty?
5. How would you describe the spirit of the feminine mission?

Further Research

By investigating the descriptions of women mentioned in the Bible, we can begin to learn the significance of the feminine mission in human relationships. Fewer than two hundred women are named in Scripture. Why were those women mentioned? In some instances you may have to follow their family trees to discover the negative or positive consequences of their relationships. An initial reference is given, which may lead you to further references. Notice not only clues to what each woman did but the actions of others

The Celebration of Womanhood

whom she influenced. You may wish to divide the following list into groups of no more than five for each woman to look up and share her research with the group later.

Name	*Reference*	*Model of/Mentor to*
Abijah	2 Kings 18:12	
Abiah	1 Chronicles 2:24	
Abigail (1)	1 Samuel 25:3	
Abigail (2)	1 Chronicles 2:15–16	
Abihail	1 Chronicles 2:29	
Abishag	1 Kings 1:13	
Abitail	2 Samuel 3:4	
Acsah	Joshua 15:16	
Adah (1)	Genesis 4:19	
Adah (2)	1 Samuel 25:43	
Ahinoam (1)	1 Samuel 14:50	
Ahinoam (2)	1 Samuel 25:43	
Aholah (Oholah)	Ezekiel 23:4	
Aholibah (Oholibac)	Ezekiel 23:4	
Aholibamah (Oholibamah)	Genesis 36:2	
Anah	Genesis 36:2	
Anna	Luke 2:36–37	
Apphia	Philemon 2	
Asenath	Genesis 41:45	
Atarah	1 Chronicles 2:26	
Athaliah	2 Kings 8:26	
Azubah (1)	1 Chronicles 2:18	
Azubah (2)	1 Kings 22:42	
Baara	1 Chronicles 8:8	
Basemath (1)	Genesis 26:34	

A Choice of Honor

Name	*Reference*	*Model of/Mentor to*
Basemath (2)	Genesis 36:23	
Bath-sheba	2 Samuel 11:3, 27	
Bernice	Acts 25:13	
Bilhah	Genesis 29:29	
Candace	Acts 8:27	
Chloe	1 Corinthians 1:11	
Claudia	2 Timothy 4:21	
Cozbi	Numbers 25:15–18	
Damaris	Acts 17:34	
Deborah (1)	Genesis 35:8	
Deborah (2)	Judges 4:4–10	
Delilah	Judges 16:45	
Dinah	Genesis 30:21	
Dorcas	Acts 9:36	
Drusilla	Acts 24:24	
Eglah	2 Samuel 3:5	
Elisabeth	Luke 1:5, 13	
Elisheba	Exodus 6:23	
Ephah	1 Chronicles 2:46	
Ephrath	1 Chronicles 2:19	
Esther	Esther 2:16–17	
Eunice	2 Timothy 1:5	
Euodia	Philippians 4:2	
Eve	Genesis 3:20	
Gomer	Hosea 1:2–6	
Hagar	Genesis 16:1	
Haggith	2 Samuel 3:4	
Hammoleketh	1 Chronicles 7:18	
Hamutal	2 Kings 23:31	
Hannah	1 Samuel 1:20	

The Celebration of Womanhood

Name	*Reference*	*Model of/Mentor to*
Hazzelelponi	1 Chronicles 4:3	
Helah	1 Chronicles 4:5	
Hephzibah	2 Kings 21:1	
Herodias	Matthew 14:36	
Hodesh	1 Chronicles 8:9	
Hoglah	Numbers 26:33	
Huldah	2 Kings 22:14	
Hushim	1 Chronicles 8:8–11	
Iscah	Genesis 11:29	
Jael	Judges 4:17	
Jecholiah	2 Kings 15:12	
Jedidah	2 Kings 22:1	
Jehoaddin	2 Kings 14:2	
Jemimah	Job 42:14	
Jerioth	1 Chronicles 2:18	
Jerusha	2 Kings 15:33	
Jezebel	1 Kings 16:30–31	
Joanna	Luke 8:3	
Jochebed	Exodus 6:20	
Judith	Genesis 26:34	
Julia	Romans 16:15	
Keren-Happuch	Job 42:14	
Keturah	Genesis 25:1	
Keziah	Job 42:14	
Leah	Genesis 29:16–30	
Lois	2 Timothy 1:5	
Lydia	Acts 16:14	
Maachah (1)	Genesis 22:23–24	
Maachah (2)	2 Samuel 3:3	

A Choice of Honor

Name	*Reference*	*Model of/Mentor to*
Maachah (3)	1 Kings 15:2	
Maachah (4)	1 Kings 15:9–10	
Maachah (5)	1 Chronicles 2:48	
Maachah (6)	1 Chronicles 7:16	
Maachah (7)	1 Chronicles 8:29	
Mahalath (1)	Genesis 28:9	
Mahalath (2)	2 Chronicles 11:18	
Mahlah	Numbers 26:33	
Martha	Luke 10:38–40; John 11:1–45	
Mary (1)	Matthew 1:16	
Mary (2)	Matthew 27:56–61	
Mary (3)	Luke 10:39	
Mary (4)	John 19:25	
Mary (5)	Acts 12:12	
Mary (6)	Romans 16:6	
Matred	Genesis 36:39	
Mehetabel	Genesis 36:39	
Merab	1 Samuel 14:49	
Meshullemeth	2 Kings 21:19	
Milcah (1)	Genesis 11:29	
Milcah (2)	Numbers 26:33	
Miriam (1)	Exodus 15:20	
Miriam (2)	1 Chronicles 4:17	
Naamah (1)	Genesis 4:22	
Naamah (2)	1 Kings 14:21	
Naarah	1 Chronicles 4:5	
Naomi	Ruth 1:2, 20	
Nehushta	2 Kings 24:8	
Noadiah	Nehemiah 6:14	

The Celebration of Womanhood

Name	*Reference*	*Model of/Mentor to*
Noah	Numbers 26:33	
Orpah	Ruth 1:4	
Peninnah	1 Samuel 1:2	
Persis	Romans 16:12	
Phoebe	Romans 16:12	
Priscilla	Acts 18:2	
Puah	Exodus 1:15	
Rachael	Genesis 29:28–32	
Rahab	Joshua 2:13	
Reumah	Genesis 22:24	
Rhoda	Acts 12:13	
Rizpah	2 Samuel 3:7	
Ruth	Ruth 1:4	
Salome	Mark 16:1	
Sapphira	Acts 5:1	
Sarah (Sarai)	Genesis 11:29	
Serah	Genesis 46:17	
Shelomith (1)	Leviticus 24:11	
Shelomith (2)	1 Chronicles 3:19	
Sheerah	1 Chronicles 7:24	
Shimeath	2 Chronicles 24:26	
Shimrith	2 Chronicles. 24:26	
Shiphrah	Exodus 1:15	
Shua	1 Chronicles 7:32	
Susanna	Luke 8:3	
Syntyche	Philippians 4:2	
Tabitha	Acts 9:36	
Tahpenes	1 Kings 11:19	
Tamar (1)	Genesis 38:6	
Tamar (2)	2 Samuel 13:1	

Name	*Reference*	*Model of/Mentor to*
Tamar (3)	2 Samuel 14:27	
Taphath	1 Kings 4:11	
Terah	Genesis 11:24	
Timna	Genesis 36:12	
Tryphena	Romans 16:12	
Tryphosa	Romans 16:12	
Vashti	Esther 1:9	
Zebidah	2 Kings 23:36	
Zeresh	Esther 5:10	
Zeruah	1 Kings 11:26	
Zeruiah	2 Samuel 17:25	
Zibiah	2 Kings 12:1	
Zillah	Genesis 4:19	
Zilpah	Genesis 29:24	
Zipporah	Exodus 2:21	

Notes

1. *The Daughters of Sarah* (May-June 1988), 47.22.

4

A Choice of Heart

[Her] heart is secure, [s]he will have no fear.
Psalm 112:8

So what is the feminine mission?

Lorraine didn't ask in so many words, but I knew that was what bothered her. She and Lawrence, her husband of four decades, had worked hard to build a comfortable life for themselves. Her commitment had paid off, she thought. She had it all—loyal children and grandchildren, a respected position in the community, and all the material possessions she could ever want. Her closet was filled with shoes from Portugal, dresses from Paris, and coats from London.

Still she communicated a restless spirit. She was a woman on the edge, unsatisfied with her circumstances, uncertain of her mission.

One evening we were seated at a dinner with Lorraine and Lawrence. As she leaned toward me in a confidential pose, her heavy gold jewels made a slight tinkling sound as if to announce her words.

"You know," she began her complaint. Then with a carefully controlled voice she critically appraised Lawrence. She was trying again to win her husband over with her reasoning. She was righteous and moral. He was wrong and immoral. Her words flew through the air like one verbal arrow after another.

I had the strange sensation that the room was still, but in reality the elegant banquet hall was a picture of gracious movement.

The Celebration of Womanhood

"Lorraine, not tonight," began Lawrence.

Why? I silently wondered. Why does she exude such a turbulent spirit?

Lorraine was committed to wholehearted living. She was a good woman, and she believed it was her mission to make her husband good, like her. Of course, it pained her to see Lawrence erring from the truth. She loved him. Why shouldn't she help him?

Lorraine was not the first woman to sabotage her mission while trying to be sincerely helpful. Her idea of help was to change—something like the "control to be like me." That was Eve's problem. And we know what her idea of help led to—the Fall.

A Mission Unlimited

Though our mission affects our relationship with people, the purpose is not to control or reform people. If we focus on people as our mission, we will eventually begin to relate to them as objects, forever trying to protect and perfect them. Think about what happens to a woman who sees her students, her employees, her neighbors, her children, or her husband as her "mission." I have been with women who began conversations with me, showing great personal interest and then slowly revealed that their interest in me was their "ministry." I was not a person to them but a mission. I also remember the experience of a relative who moved to Mexico with her husband to fulfill a professorial assignment at the university. Lonely and experiencing culture shock, she occasionally sought out the fellowship of another American woman in the neighborhood, a missionary. One morning as my relative knocked at her door, the missionary stayed behind the screen and explained, "I can't talk to you. My mission is to the Mexican people, not American people."

A Choice of Heart

Unfortunately, in looking at people—specifically Mexican people—as her mission, that woman had made them into objects that she would change. In that limited view of mission, she could selectively control the people to whom she ministered.

Although our mission affects our relationships with people, its function is not to reform or control people. It is equally important to notice that though our mission affects the marriage relationship, it is not limited to the marriage relationship. As we will see later, an unmarried woman was created for the same mission as a married woman.

A Mission of Life

Ruth was a woman who stayed in the center of life and was empowered to celebrate her mission even when her circumstances pressured her to give up and sit on the sidelines.

An economic depression had caused a number of families to move to cities that promised a better financial picture. That is how Ruth met her future husband and her in-laws. They had moved to her area looking for a better life. They were a close family of four—a mother, father, and two brothers.

Difficult as it was to leave their roots, the move proved to be a good decision. The family settled into their new home and made friends in the community. Ruth met them and was especially attracted to one of the young men. They fell in love.

Ruth's life changed dramatically in the next few years. First there was the great joy of love and marriage, mixed with the sadness of her father-in-law's death. Her husband's brother also married, another change that called for celebration.

Time passed quickly as the two young couples and the widowed mother grew closer. Almost ten years passed.

The Celebration of Womanhood

Then old wounds of grief were reopened when Ruth's husband and his brother died. In the turbulence of their loss, the three women clung together.

It was Ruth's behavior during troubled times that made her story famous. She found a way to celebrate in every circumstance. When her mother-in-law decided to return to her roots, where her relatives were living and where she still owned some land, Ruth said, "Let's go." Though Naomi tried to discourage her, she couldn't. Ruth's purpose, or mission, did not die with her loved ones. Her mission was a mission of life. No matter how drastically her circumstances changed, she continued to confirm her purpose and celebrate.

A Mission of Purpose

As we look closely at the book of Ruth and compare it with other Scriptures, we see a practical demonstration of what the feminine mission is, what it means, and how we celebrate.

Five goals are distinguished in the feminine mission:

Goal	*Primary Reference*	*Example*
to create communion	Genesis 2:18–24	Ruth 1:4, 16–17
to inspire vision and hope	Genesis 3:20 1 Peter 3:1, 8	Ruth 2:2, 11–12
to do right without fear	1 Peter 3:5–6	Ruth 3
to affirm and sustain life	Genesis 1:28; 3:20	Ruth 4:13, 15
to reflect glory (unfading beauty)	1 Corinthians 11:7 1 Peter 3:1–6	Ruth 4:14–15

Communion

Fellowship, wholeness, companionship, support, encouragement, honest interaction—all of those are a part of communion. Communion also means a oneness of spirit with another and in marriage extends to a physical oneness. Woman was created with a unique capacity for communion that brings completeness to man and in a broader sphere emotionally and spiritually extends to society.

Vision

The very name of Eve means "fullness of life," implying something beyond giving birth. A full life is filled with hope and vision. A woman's intuitive capacity gives her a distinct opportunity to inspire hope and vision in others.

Righteousness

Righteousness is doing what is right, good, and pure without fear. Though man is equally responsible for this goal, it is of particular significance for woman in understanding the relationship of submission to the feminine mission.

Life

Life, although also declared as a responsibility of both man and woman, is of particular significance as a woman faces complex questions about life and death, health, and the physical environment.

Glory

The purity of glory (as opposed to disgrace) and the genuineness of beauty (of the inner self) are qualities that a woman develops by putting her hope in God.

You may ask, *Why focus on the illustration of Ruth?* Can married women find benefit in the story of a single woman? It is because of the assumption that the mission differs for different women that we are intentionally studying the story of Ruth—to demonstrate that our mission is the same, regardless of status or circumstances.

It is primarily in our interpersonal relationships that we pursue our mission, yet we must remember that our focus is not on controlling a person but rather on creating communion, inspiring vision, doing right, affirming life, and reflecting glory. What a difference that focus makes. It frees us to peacefully and positively interact together, regardless of the failure of others. It frees us to confront wrong, be angry and not sin, lead and, yes, even choose to submit.

To follow the feminine mission we must get off the sidelines and actively apply our minds and hearts to the unique way in which each of us can reach those goals. That is your personal mission, and it will be distinguished by your individuality. You will carry the ball and run a little differently than others in the game, even though your purpose is the same.

A Mission of Power

Let's be realistic. How can we reach our goals when discrimination and abuse still exist? The secret of empowerment is in understanding and applying the principles of commitment power, communication power, and confirmation power. See the chart on the next page.

Three commonly used words—commitment, submission, and hope—are the keys to empowerment in the feminine mission. The first two have been overused and misused so dramatically that we shy away from them. Since negative associations are likely to come to mind in a discussion of their meaning, let us acknowledge those associations here. Let's do some brainstorming for a moment. Write down your responses. When you hear the word *commitment*, what comes to mind? Write the words that come to mind whether they make sense or not. For example: marriage, work, appointment, duty, boxed in, obligation.

THE DYNAMIC INTEGRATION OF PEOPLE WITH PRINCIPLES

You +

   Interpersonal Relationships

      + *Mission Principles*
         create communion
         inspire vision
         do right
         affirm life
         reflect glory

         + *Empowerment Principles*
            commitment power
            communication power
            confirmation power

SUSTAINED BY HOPE

Now try the same exercise with the word *submission*. What do you imagine? Beating, humbling, lesser, prison, giving up? Perhaps most of our immediate associations are negative. We are conditioned by the abuse of those words to resist them.

Briefly, try an experiment with me. Take the paper with your answers and seal it in an envelope. Determine to leave your feelings and past experiences with commitment and submission in the envelope while you complete this chapter. We need to agree upon an authentic, positive meaning for each of those words.

Commitment

Commitment is often referred to as a character quality. "She's a committed person," we say. For the true meaning of commitment we must examine what one is committed to. The value of the object of commitment reflects back to the one making the commitment and gives value to your action.

As an action, commitment becomes the effort to integrate your will with an ideal or another individual's will, and the work you do to bring good to something or someone outside of yourself.

Fear is what tempts you to open your envelope of negative associations concerning commitment. You may fear that your action of commitment will cause you to lose your individuality. Will your allegiance to a person or group, or to God, take away your identity?

The answer lies in an understanding of pure submission.

Submission

Is *submission* an antiquated word with no positive meaning in our culture today? If you think that this question is irrelevant, please bear with me. I, too, am appalled by the definition of this word today. It makes it difficult to even consider an unadulterated meaning. However, a clear understanding is essential to understanding the dynamic of commitment power.

Pure submission describes the positive action of serious and respectful commitment, the direct opposite of abusive subjugation. Sin causes man to turn the purpose of pure submission inside out; dominating, humiliating, and enslaving women does not lead to submission.

Respectful commitment as referred to in 1 Peter 3 involves a positive action of voluntary yielding in love.[1] Rather than losing your identity as an individual, you gain freedom and power.

In *Celebration of Discipline*, Richard J. Foster writes, "In submission we are at last free to value other people. . . . We have entered into a new, wonderful, glorious free-

A Choice of Heart

dom, the freedom to give up our rights for the good of others."[2]

Peter encourages that kind of respectful commitment. His examples reflect the positive result of doing right without fear:

	Act of Respectful Commitment	*Result*
1 Peter 2:13	Submit . . . to authority	It will silence ignorant talk of foolish men
1 Peter 2:17	Show proper respect	You represent God
1 Peter 2:21	Entrust as Christ did	You are healed by His wounds
1 Peter 3:1–6	Wives . . . submit	Husbands will be won

Respectful commitment recognizes the responsibility of authority and respects the right of that authority to succeed or fail.

If you resent or resist the idea of submission, it may be that you have lost sight of your purpose. A student respectfully commits herself to doing what the teacher says for the purpose of learning (and a good grade). An employee respectfully commits herself to the authority of her boss because she realizes the company runs smoother when employees honor the chain-of-command. Both voluntarily submit to the authority of another for a higher purpose, not necessarily because the authority is always right.

So respectful commitment is not to be confused with the erroneous models of submission in the soap operas and eccentric sects portrayed by the media.

Submission without commitment. Submission without commitment leads to enslavement and destruction of self-esteem. Submission without commitment is also manipulative and devastating to one or both parties. That is what happens in the situation of a man and woman who live together without the commitment of marriage. Submission to intimacy without the power of commitment sets up the same relational dynamics as enslavement. Such a giving-withholding relationship is selfish and suffocating to spiritual growth. It is defrauding to one or both parties and strangles emotional growth. And it defiles the laws of purity, often scarring physical growth.

It is confusion about the relationship between commitment and submission that elicits the cry of complaint about patriarchy.

Commitment without submission. Commitment without submission limits the nature of a relationship and confines its potential. It is the respect displayed in submissive commitment that allows a personal relationship to grow.

Commitment with mutual submission. If you believe that women carry an unfair burden in commitment, look at the rigorous standard for a man listed in Ephesians 5:22–33: He must sacrifice self; love his wife as Christ loved the church; give himself to her as pure, holy, and blameless; love and provide for her as for his own body.

The ideal, then, is the balance of mutual giving and loving. In this sense, the commitment is to mutual submission "out of reverence for Christ" (Ephesians 5:21).

Principle of Commitment Power

As the dynamic action of commitment becomes integrated with your energies, intellect, and will, you will be empowered to celebrate the feminine mission. This principle may be illustrated by examining the empowering effect of the four following commitments:

A Choice of Heart

1. A commitment to God, or a personal relationship with Jesus Christ, is the only one that can promise redemption from sins and release from the power of evil. Without submissive commitment to God, one quickly runs out of power to sustain other commitments.
2. The second commitment is the commitment to God in single life. As a single woman entrusts her entire being to God, He restores and empowers her to live a pure and positive life. As she learns to "do what is right and . . . not give way to fear," she will be blessed by "the beauty of a gentle and quiet spirit, which is of great worth in God's sight" (1 Peter 3:6, 4).
3. The third commitment is the commitment to God and husband in marriage. The reciprocal respect and confidence generated by the intimate submission commitment in marriage energizes a woman in her relationship with her husband and with others.
4. The fourth commitment is the commitment to a fellowship of believers. Through this commitment a woman can become more confident and energized in her family and in social relationships as a model and mentor. Her relationship to the body of believers is strengthened as she participates in the encouragement of growth and the acknowledgment of responsibility and respect for leadership.

As a result:

- Others are magnetically drawn to her commitments, and she is empowered in the marketplace.
- She is renewed and empowered within as she continues to seek knowledge and understanding.
- As she reaches out to women on the edge, she is empowered by wisdom to hear and to heal.

The Celebration of Womanhood

The discipline of commitment must be continually renewed to experience empowered celebration. The secret that urges us to this renewal is hope. Ruth never lost her hope. In contrast, Naomi found it so difficult to cope that her friends did not even recognize her when she returned home.

"Can this be Naomi?" they exclaimed.

"Don't call me Naomi," she told them. "Call me Mara, because the Almighty has made my life very bitter. I went away full, but the Lord has brought me back empty. Why call me Naomi?" (Ruth 1:19–21).

Though Ruth suffered, she continued to look forward. Her secret was knowing that hope is more than an emotion. She exercised the action of hope as she consistently put her expectations for each person and circumstance in a safe, secure place. If her hope rested in a situation, a possession, or a person, it could be lost or abused. If she put her hope in herself, she would discover moments of weakness or failure. She put her hope in God, again and again, confidently continuing in the center of life without fear.

Paul explains the process of placing one's hope in God in his letter that speaks to Euodia and Syntyche. "Take your requests—your problems, circumstances—and seal them in an envelope," he says, in effect. "Then place your hope for the resolution of those problems in God's hands. And don't forget to thank Him. When you do this, the peace of God that transcends all understanding will guard your hearts and your minds, freeing you to think about what is true, noble, right, pure, lovely, admirable, excellent, and praiseworthy" (see Philippians 4).

How Do We Celebrate?

In chapter 1 we noted the questions that are raised by women on the edge. Are we human, equal, worthy, significant, redeemed? When a woman struggles with stress, discrimination, gender abuse, and the enervating push and pull of daily interpersonal relationships, she has a choice. She can remain on the sidelines, or she can decide to search for knowledge and understanding of her mission. That is a choice of the mind.

As she searches for truth, she will discover both real and false leadership. If she is sincere in her search she will follow the source of integrity. That is the choice of honor.

In order to celebrate she must make a move, take a risk, step away from the edge, and get into the action on the field. No matter what position she plays, her mission must be constantly in view. The secret of her success and celebration is directly related to her source of power. Just as commitment power is necessary for her initial involvement, it must be continually renewed in order to carry on. That power infuses her as she commits herself to ideals and individuals, putting her hope or expectations in God alone. Notice how Ruth was empowered to pursue the goals of the feminine mission.

The Goal of Communion

Ruth's hope in God empowered her to keep her commitment to Naomi to move to a foreign land, creating communion and support and giving companionship.

The Goal of Vision

Ruth's hope in God empowered her to follow a commitment of vision and venture out among strangers to work in the fields. Her actions were noted favorably by Boaz.

The Goal of Doing Right

Ruth's hope in God empowered her to risk her future for the sake of a greater good for both herself and Naomi.

The Goal of Affirming and Sustaining Life

Ruth's hope in God empowered her to make a commitment to new life (she became a mother) and to renew and sustain older life (by unselfishly sharing the joy and care of her son with Naomi).

The Goal of Glory

Ruth's hope in God empowered her to keep her commitments and reflect the beauty and glory of God with gentleness and a quiet spirit.

The woman who puts her hope in God without fear knows that this is a choice of the heart.

Discovering Your Mission

1. Why do you think a person should not be your mission?
2. How do the goals of your mission allow you to celebrate even when people disappoint you?
3. What is the difference between mission principles and empowerment principles?
4. How does submission relate to commitment?

Further Research

Peter refers to a "gentle and quiet spirit" (1 Peter 3:4). Why do you think that is included in the discussion of beauty? To probe their meaning, study the roots of those words and compare their use in other Scriptures.

It is not often that we think of someone as having that quality. I saw the beauty of spirit in the face of my friend Joyce Erickson, who began celebrating in heaven in August 1993. As you read the following, think of the relationship of a quiet spirit to commitment and the feminine mission.

A Choice of Heart

Joyce	*Mission Accomplished*
My friend always restores my spirit.	Inspired hope and vision
I am drawn to her words of warm wisdom.	Encouraged to do right
She is always at peace.	Reflected glory
I am drawn by the calm of her listening.	Created communion
My friend always sees hope in God.	Reflected glory
I am drawn by her purity of heart.	Displayed righteousness
She is still though surrounded by a storm.	Doing right without fear
I am drawn to her quiet spirit.	Reflected glory

How does this example relate to the references in 1 Peter 3 and Psalm 131?

Notes

1. George W. Knight, Dean and Professor at Knox Theological Seminary, in John Piper and Wayne A. Grudem, eds. *Recovering Biblical Manhood & Womanhood* (Wheaton, Ill.: Crossway, 1991), 166.
2. Richard J. Foster, *Celebration of Discipline* (San Francisco: Harper & Row, 1978), 98.

5

A Choice of Triumph

In the end [s]he will look in triumph.

Psalm 112:8

I was twenty-eight the summer Raye and I met again. We had been friends for a dozen and a half years.

As she came through the door, a fresh, familiar feeling filled the room. It was if we were ten years old again, sitting cross-legged on the grass in her backyard. A hedge shielded us from the outside world. It provided a secure shelter for our private talks.

As we did at age ten, we continued at twenty-eight to talk vigorously about everything. We were best friends. We shared a love for learning, laughing, and imagining how the world would be as we grew older. Our minds were full. Our hearts were warm.

On that visit, however, I realized that our friendship was changing. We were stretching and reaching out to new experiences, intrigued and stimulated by new knowledge, pushing and pulling in different directions.

Raye was faithfully communicating and confirming her mission. Though she never abandoned her faith, she began to question the faithful. She was justifiably frustrated by people who presented "spiritual" solutions before listening to or living through problems.

I knew how she felt. I had once worked in a ministry where a temporary volunteer whooshed into our lives and out again, counseling and controlling conversations, leaving

The Celebration of Womanhood

many people feeling anxious and confused behind her. I was sensitive to the problem Raye was facing. She was determined not to articulate disconnected answers to distressed people. She would listen to them and apply her mind to sensitive solutions.

Raye began to interpret the Bible in view of her own experiences. Some passages appeared restrictive and harsh to her. As she tried to balance the voices of the social activists with scholarly and spiritual voices, she loosened her grip on her traditional roots and gravitated toward social activism in the ghetto.

How do we continue our pursuit of the feminine mission when confronted with the pressure to be compassionate, safe, and satisfied? How do we separate cultural and biblical imperatives?

Hearing Notes of Discord

Raye heard the dissonant notes of intellectual and emotional experiences shouting from the real-world collage of feminine life, often distorting the music and true meaning of her existence. Women unable to balance the following voices are more vulnerable to the entrapment and destructiveness of the world.

Low Self-Esteem

Lack of self-esteem can lead to underachievement, xenophobia (fear of strangers), depression, and suicide.

Confusion of Identity

This is may lead to the promotion of androgyny, transsexualism, transvestitism, homosexuality, lesbianism, and substance abuse.

Mental and Physical Abuse

This is apparent in sexual harassment, mental cruelty, and physical torture.

Friction with Men

This can lead to misogamy (hatred of marriage), misogyny (hatred of women), and misanthropy (hatred of humankind).

The pressures caused by these problems devastate relationships and elevate the feminist cry for justice and empowerment. And the cycle of voices begin again, pushing us to the edge. It is common to hear them urging:

"Compromise!"
"Channel!"
"Let go! Let God!"
"Keep the faith!"
"Submit!"
"Be aggressive!"
"Let everyone go her own way!"

How can a woman sort out these conflicting messages? Where is the sound of wisdom among the voices?

Raye lived in the city with real, struggling, but surviving people. As she sacrificed the security of her future, the serenity of her family, and ultimately her marriage, she responded to many opposing and confusing voices calling women to be all they were meant to be. What did she hear? What voices do we hear that complicate our thinking and cause some to abandon hope?

Auditioning New Voices

The Presumptuous Voice

The presumptuous voice calls, "Be subject to men because they were given divine power over women." That idea comes from the erroneous conclusion that some have drawn from the Genesis account of the Fall. God confronted Adam and Eve with their responsibilities: she would desire to control and cover for Adam, but God would hold Adam responsible. Thus began the rumor that God said that men should have power over women. That view persists in some cultures today.

Anne Wilson Schaef, psychotherapist and founder of the Women's Institute of Alternative Psychotherapy, wrote about the power and influence of white males in our society in what she calls the White Male System.[1] She stated that a white woman's identity comes from the White Male System that controls our culture and that the White Male System validates that identity.

Could the assumption be true that, in our society, even unaware of its origin, men and women have stretched the meaning of Genesis to say that they have power that defines God—god-power? Those who applaud "the White Male System" are abusing God's design for relationships.

The Scholarly Voice

The scholarly voice says, "Women are equally redeemed and therefore equal in authority with men." There are two truths here that tend to confuse us. First is the truth of redemption. Second is the truth of the equality of man and woman.

In *Women in the Maze,* Ruth Tucker writes, "The effects of the curse on man and woman are not irreversible."[2] Her argument is confusing because the reader is led to believe that woman's commitment to man was an effect of the curse, which can be negated through redemption.

At the same time Tucker states, "Those who emphasize male headship often use the 'curse' as a strong argument for their case."³ The implication is that male headship was instituted, if not as a curse, as a result of Eve's sin.

But that would mean that redemption eliminated headship. One might then conclude that submission-commitment is a negative, an afterthought, a punishment. Is that consistent with Scripture?

The Cunning Voice

The cunning voice coos, "A submissive woman is manipulative." Many story lines in the media portray a submissive character as weak or manipulative. Either way it is offensive.

The advice of secular psychologist Dr. Toni Grant in *Being a Woman* is that we should understand and accept the role we play as women. Dr. Grant examines the four characters women portray in life: the Madonna, the Mother, the Amazon, or the Courtesan.⁴ In essence she says that we will be happier if we learn to submit to our unique role as women. Some confuse her view with that of the feminine mission. But it is not the same. Our mission involves a focus on others, yet Grant's submission is defined by a focus on self, accepting the assignment of one's character as a duty for the purpose of ultimate self-satisfaction.

That approach to submissive behavior is narcissistic and manipulative, and it seriously damages the balance of relationships.

The Fearful Voice

The fearful voice warns, "Women who support men will experience abuse."

Women who have observed or experienced abuse may have great difficulty discussing the subject of commitment and submission in relationships. Are we listening to those women? What do we communicate to them? Are our words condemning or comforting?

The Celebration of Womanhood

It is callous and supercilious to deny the reality of women's suffering. But how does one counterbalance the claim that all women will have the same experience? Before we counsel others, we need to understand the seriousness and significance of the feminine mission.

The Politically Correct Voice

The politically correct voice instructs, "A distinct feminine mission is inappropriate for our times and culture." This is a complex issue because it involves not only a careful determination of one's approach to Scripture but a serious commitment to understanding its universal application to life.

If you reject the concept of the biblical feminine mission as inappropriate for our times and culture, are you rejecting the biblical meaning itself or a distorted application of it? Are you putting your cultural experience first and applying it to the Word of God? Or are you honestly looking to the authority of God and asking Him to apply His Word to your experience?

The Religious Voice

The literature of Christian authors reveals heartbreaking stories of more hurt than healing precipitated by the struggle of women and men deliberating over feminine issues. It is time to look beyond the debate regarding ministry and minding your husband, and discover the significance of the feminine mission.

I agree with Raye that we must know and seek to understand the real women in the world—in the cities or suburbs and in the countryside. What can we do when we see dissension and discrimination around us?

The Melody of Godly Wisdom

We must listen to the voice of wisdom as we celebrate the feminine mission. The sage King Solomon encouraged us to search for wisdom with the same intensity that we would apply in looking for silver and hidden treasure. And we are promised: "Then you will understand the fear of the Lord and find the knowledge of God. For the Lord gives wisdom, and from His mouth come knowledge and understanding" (Proverbs 2:5–6).

Though I like the "search" feature on the local library computer, it does not require the same passion as the search for silver and gold. It allows the user to type a request for a particular book or author or the name of a subject, and the computer searches for all the books and magazines that address that subject. If you push the right buttons it will even provide a summary of the contents of each reference.

But searching goes beyond mere looking. The search for wisdom requires both desire and discipline. Searching involves intense and eternal looking, and as a successful action it involves listening. Whether I am looking for a book or for silver, when I find it I will examine it and meditate on it.

The culmination of my searching is learning to live with what I have found. Should that be a part of my life? How can I understand it? Solomon writes, "If you call out for insight and cry aloud for understanding . . . you will understand. . . . Discretion will protect you" (Proverbs 2:3, 9, 11).

A wisdom checklist might look like this:

The Celebration of Womanhood

Wisdom Search

- *Looking*
  make intensive search
  keep your eyes open for little treasures
- *Examining*
  question and listen
  meditate
- *Understanding*
  knowledge will be pleasant
  discretion will protect you
  understanding will guard you

Though the voice of wisdom sounds sedate and scholarly, it holds the secret to knowing and understanding and doing what is good and right and fair. Queen Esther, the beautiful Jewish woman who saved her people from annihilation, actualized that secret. She searched for knowledge and wisdom, and she pursued her mission, affirming life, empowered by her commitment, and sustained by hope in God. How she communicated that wisdom was the secret to her success. She communicated with discretion.

That is what Raye was asking for—discernment, or discretion. Knowledge may be stored in the head, understanding developed by experience, but wisdom comes from God. It is wisdom that energizes discretion.

Discretion is the practical side of wisdom. Discretion acts out of concern for another before self. Discretion will protect you. We are told: "Pay attention to my wisdom, listen well to my words of insight, that you may maintain discretion and your lips may preserve knowledge" (Proverbs 5:1–2).

Wisdom and discretion are the keys to triumph in the feminine mission.

Discovering Your Mission

1. What obstacles do you face in following the feminine mission?
2. Observe how the voices of opposing views are suggested to us in the media, in literature, and through educational sources and politics. Write down your observations, and comment on specific areas: presumptuous voices, scholarly voices, cunning voices, politically correct voices, and religious voices.

Further Research

Read the book of Esther in one sitting, noting specific words and actions that reveal her understanding of the feminine mission. Relate her situation to a similar modern circumstance.

NOTES

1. Anne Wilson Schaef, *Women's Reality: An Emerging Female System in the White Male Society* (Minneapolis: Winston, 1981).
2. Ruth A. Tucker, *Women in the Maze: Questions and Answers on Biblical Equality* (Downers Grove, Ill.: InterVarsity, 1992), 53.
3. Ibid., 51.
4. Toni Grant, *Being a Woman: Fulfilling Your Femininity and Finding Love* (New York: Random, 1988).

Part Two

COMMUNICATION POWER

The Principle of Communication Power

As you develop communication skills in creating communion, giving hope and vision, affirming life, doing what is right without fear, and reflecting glory, you will be empowered to celebrate the feminine mission.

The Biblical Models of Communication Power

The women and men of Thessalonica dynamically model the principle of communication power, dramatically displaying hope in their speech and conduct.

6
Communications that Promote Communion

*He who answers before listening—
that is his folly and his shame.*

Proverbs 18:13

Gracie leaned her cherubic face close to mine and pressed her tiny four-year-old hands against my cheeks. "Mommy, listen to me with your face," she pleaded.

As speakers or listeners we communicate multiple nonverbal messages with our faces. Gracie knew she was not getting my full attention unless I "listened with my face."

Think about it. It is face-to-face communication that leads to oneness and fellowship, to communion. The concept of face-to-face communication implies an interchange of speaking and listening, observing.

The psalmist asked the Lord, "Hear us . . . make your face shine upon us" (Psalm 80:1, 3).

Paul spoke face-to-face with a small group of Thessalonians, and he later commended them as models of positive, interactive communication. They didn't just hear his words; they "received" them and accepted them as the truth, taking action—trusting, risking, respecting, supporting and encouraging, submitting to common goals, and reflecting the glory of Christ. They were committed to Paul's team. In our pursuit of the feminine mission, particularly as we seek to create communion, we will be empowered in our communication as we model the same actions as ingredients of teamwork.

The Celebration of Womanhood

Trust is essential for fellowship and oneness, and it is the key to affirming life. Without it the concept of teamwork is a facade for selfishness. In chapter 7 we will further explore the ingredient of trust in communication.

In the automotive industry, team training workshops include an exercise called "the faith fall." Falling backward, each team member must trust the rest of the team to catch him or her. Though that may appear to be a physical exercise, the psychological implications are clear. Risk, like the faith fall, is the ultimate demonstration of trust, and the feminine mission is not without risk.

Submission to common goals is desirable in seeking solutions to conflict. It is the only way a team can work. This key to a woman's continual pursuit of her mission will be the focus of chapter 9.

Unfading beauty and glory are the result of teamwork and communion. The often misunderstood comment of Paul that "woman is the glory of man" (1 Corinthians 11:7) is actually a positive affirmation of a woman's relationship as a teammate with her husband.

Renowned theologian J. Sidlow Baxter writes, "Paul is the champion of woman's liberation, and it is tragic that he has been so misinterpreted." Concerning 1 Corinthians 11 he continues, "All Paul's counsels in this chapter are safeguards of Christian womanhood, not prison chains!"[1]

Though the components of interactive communications that facilitate teamwork overlap, as do our actions in pursuit of our mission, we will consider their application to our listening and response patterns in this chapter and the application to our language usage in chapter 8.

How Listening Creates Communion

Sue is a woman who listens. No matter how full her schedule, she makes others feel that their words are worthy of her consideration. She is willing to put aside routine for the sake of a relationship. It was that unselfish, inclusive attitude that first drew me to her in 1972.

She was a busy wife and mother, active in church and school and caring for relatives in the community, but our spontaneous meetings were joyful and invigorating because of her understanding heart. Because she was willing to listen face-to-face, soon we began to share heart-to-heart.

By Showing You Care

Sue not only heard me but tangibly empathized with me, and it was her empathy that moved her to action. On many occasions she not only loaned me her car and shared family dinners with us, but she also kept my children overnight and even helped me clean my house. When you listen, you restore honor by showing esteem for another, showing empathy for another, and encouraging another.

By Showing Honor

Sue listens in a way that restores self-esteem. I have never heard her promote herself as a great listener or say, "I'll listen. It's my gift." Such a statement is patronizing and stresses the importance of the listener rather than genuine interest in the speaker.

When someone like Sue listens she empties her head of self and focuses on her friend. We are all encouraged by friends who listen that way. It is such friends whom we treasure, who know us the best, who can give us the most useful feedback.

The discipline of respectful listening as modeled by the Thessalonians is rewarding. Do you honor the words of all humanity equally, or do you interrupt, prejudge, or push away? There are no conditions on the commandment "Honor one another above yourselves." In fact, the Scripture emphasizes:

The Celebration of Womanhood

> Bless those who persecute you; bless and do not curse. . . . Live in harmony with one another. Do not be proud, but be willing to associate with people of low position. Do not be conceited. Do not repay anyone evil for evil. Be careful to do what is right in the eyes of everybody. If it is possible, as far as it depends on you, live at peace with everyone. Do not take revenge, my friends. (Romans 12:14-19)

As a woman, I learned from the model of a man, my husband, that the concept of honor in listening should apply to our children as well as adults. Even when they were very young, he showed his value for them as individuals by respecting their privacy and listening and discussing sensitive concerns alone with them. Even if their conversations involved discipline, the children knew that their words were worthwhile and that they were important to him because he was willing to take time to listen to them alone.

By Showing Encouragement

Listening that honors communicates hope and opens the door to understanding. It is this hope and understanding that brings encouragement. When you tell a friend that you would like to talk with her, you are looking for hope, not judgment. And so it is when a friend shares her heart with you. Remember that you do not need to solve your friend's problem. You show honor by waiting until specifically asked to suggest a solution. Remember that you do not need to "sympathize" with your friend by drawing the attention to yourself and emphasizing your own personal conflicts. You give hope and encouragement by standing with and standing up for those you love.

How Listening Increases Understanding

"He who answers before listening—that is his folly and

Communications that Promote Communion

his shame" (Proverbs 18:13). When you listen receptively you begin a process that draws others to listen to you. You rally another's hearing. Hearing brings knowledge, and from that knowledge comes understanding.

Listening means more than being able to repeat the words that were said. It means looking for nonverbal messages as well as the translation of sound. It means listening to the content of a message and being willing to receive new messages. Jeremiah was sent with a clear message to Judah. God's words were not new to His people. They had once followed His way and then drifted away. In His lovingkindness God sent Jeremiah to warn them that though their wickedness was splitting their relationship with Him like a divorce, He would have mercy if they returned to Him. The people heard the words, but they didn't get the message. They had no desire to understand.

God finally told Jeremiah, "Announce this to the house of Jacob and proclaim it in Judah: Hear this, you foolish and senseless people, who have eyes but do not see, who have ears but do not hear" (Jeremiah 5:21). Meaningful listening requires a decision—to pay attention, a determination—to understand, and a discipline of the mind—to interact.

It Brings Focus

Physical noise and movement are obvious distractions to listening. We naturally stop activities such as playing the piano or doing aerobics when we really want to listen. Though psychological and emotional distractions are less obvious, they are just as effective in deafening our ears to a message. Are you preoccupied with a project or problem? Are you thinking about how uncomfortable your shoes feel? Are you still mad about the traffic jam on the freeway?

When you decide to listen, try to be prepared to listen. If you are carrying a heavy bag of books, set it down. If your feet hurt, sit down. Nothing makes a speaker feel more frustrated than to observe that the other person is ill at ease, waiting to escape.

It Forces Us to Be Real

Are you a pseudolistener? In other words, do you pretend to listen? It is a well-known fact that our minds can assimilate many more words than a speaker can pronounce in one minute. It is easy to become distracted when a speaker is uncertain or redundant in his message. That is true one-on-one as well as in a group.

It Makes Us See Others

Bargaining for center stage creates another barrier to listening. If you have decided to listen, listen. Concentrate on the other person when you catch yourself programming your response in your mind before he or she has finished speaking. It is not necessary to speak immediately when the other person pauses or concludes a thought. You might say, "I hear you. Let me think about that for a moment."

Relationships begin to grow when we make a decision about listening.

How Listening Gives Hope

As you apply your heart to listening you will be moved to react honestly and still give hope. By understanding three emotions, we can learn to respond truthfully yet positively. These emotions are: sympathy, empathy, and pity.

Sympathy is a simple feeling of compassion for another person's situation. If someone breaks a leg, we sympathize with her pain and isolation. Though we are sorry for her suffering we are not personally suffering. We express sympathy from the outside looking in.

Communications that Promote Communion

Empathy moves us inside the situation with our friend. We have lost loved ones too, so we feel pain with our friend's pain. We have a deeper level of understanding and emotion because of our experience.

When we pity someone, we put ourselves in a superior position. The problem with pity is that it often separates or creates distance between people.

Which emotion, then, is the most appropriate and hopeful in a relationship? Certainly pity does not encourage growth. Although it admits to understanding, it will never let you share hope and healing. Empathy helps. It can hold you when you are hurting. It tightens the bond of heart to heart. But it can also cause you to lose perspective and keep you from encouraging growth. Sympathy is safe but somewhat stuffy.

How can we effectively determine to understand? The answer lies in not separating our ears from our hearts or mouths or eyes. How, then, does face-to-face, heart-to-heart listening help you to comprehend another?

It Opens Your Eyes

Body language reveals the attitude of a message. Sitting or standing with your arms folded across your chest is a way to distance and defend; it exhibits a wait-and-see attitude. Learn to study body language. Envision the attitudes expressed in the following gestures: a woman with her legs crossed, hands folded in lap; a man with legs crossed, hands folded in lap; a woman sitting straight, knees together, feet flat; a man leaning over a woman, arm on her shoulder; a woman leaning over man, arm on his shoulder.

Listening involves seeing what is being said as well as hearing. Body language may confirm or contradict the verbal message.

It Quickens the Ears

The pitch, tone, and volume of a message also makes a difference. A person can say, "I'm sorry," or, "I love you," in a variety of tones, volumes, and pitches that may alter their meaning. Listen for those symbols of meaning.

It Refines the Words of Your Mouth

There are two ways we can actively give encouragement as a listener. One is by paraphrasing. The other is by questioning.

Paraphrasing is the skill of re-phrasing what you are hearing and repeating it back to the speaker for verification. For instance, Liz may say, "The girls get into little cliques, and I don't know them. Do I have to go to youth group?"

You may respond, "Do I hear you saying that you don't want to go to youth group because no one makes an effort to know you and you feel ignored?"

When you paraphrase you do not add to the message or change it to match your opinion. You simply repeat in different words the message you are hearing. It gives the speaker an opportunity to change or clarify her message.

Liz may answer, "Well, it is not that I feel ignored. It's just that—well, I don't know how to talk to them."

You say, "Oh, then they're not ignoring you, but you feel left out because they are talking about something that you don't know about?"

"Yeah, that's it. They all go to the Christian school and I don't."

"Are you saying that you don't think they are snobs but you feel you're missing something because you don't go to their school?"

Though many sources of hope can temporarily inspire a woman to emulate the example of listening given by the

Thessalonians—receiving, accepting, and responding—only a woman's hope in God will empower her to endure in times of struggle and suffering.

As with the Thessalonians, the gospel comes to us "not simply in words, but also in power."

Dietrich Bonhoeffer wrote, "One who cannot listen long and patiently will presently be talking beside the point and be never really speaking to others, albeit he be not conscious of it. Anyone who thinks that his time is too valuable to spend keeping quiet will eventually have no time for God and his brother, but only for himself and for his own follies."[2]

Discovering Your Mission

1. What verbal and nonverbal messages make you feel as if someone is not listening?

2. Describe a woman you know who is a good listener. How do you feel around her?

3. Check your own listening habits. Are you easily distracted, dramatic, or dominating? Why?

4. Apply the principle of communication power, specifically in the area of listening, to teamwork.

Mission Goal	*Communication Power*	*Application*
To create communion	Respectful listening	
To give glory	Hearing with your heart	
To do right	Honest and open listening and paraphrasing	
To affirm life	Paraphrasing, integrity, symbols	
To reflect glory	Respectful listening	

Further Research

Study a biography, or through observation and research analyze the listening habits of a woman whose communications create communion. Notice how she responds in both personal and public situations. What can you learn from her?

Notes

1. J. Sidlow Baxter, *Explore the Book* (Grand Rapids: Zondervan, 1960), 6:115.
2. Dietrich Bonhoeffer, trans. John W. Doberstein, *Life Together* (New York: Harper and Brothers, 1954), 98.

7

Communications that Encourage Trust

Love is patient . . . kind . . . always hopes.
1 Corinthians 13:4, 7

Imagine the role of women living in Israel in 1050 B.C. As early as age thirteen or fourteen a girl could marry. Her husband might have another wife or two, and it was possible that she would never see her family again. In those circumstances a woman's strongest personal relationships were often with her children.

During that time a woman named Hannah was married to Elkanah. He also had another wife called Peninnah, or Penny. Their story is recorded in 1 Samuel.

Hannah loved her husband, and he loved her deeply. Polygamy was the custom, so what was her problem? She suffered from chronic depression. The other woman, Penny, had children and Hannah did not. And it wasn't enough for Penny to be happy with her children. She harassed Hannah, taunting and provoking her until she could not eat and only wanted to cry.

Elkanah couldn't understand. "Why are you weeping?" he asked Hannah. "Why don't you eat? Why are you downhearted? Don't I mean more to you than ten sons?" (1:8).

He didn't understand. He couldn't console her. It wasn't only the longing for a child but the constant harassment from Penny that pierced Hannah's heart. *How could he marry a woman like Penny?* Hannah must have wondered.

Have you ever felt confined or desperate because of decisions you or, worse yet, someone else made that you couldn't do anything about? That is how Hannah felt.

Her story might have ended there if it had not been for love. She communicated love by actions of trust, declaring to God, "If You will only look upon your servant's misery and remember me, and not forget your servant but give her a son, then I will give him to the Lord for all the days of his life, and no razor will ever be used on his head" (1:11).

How could Hannah vow to give up her child? What would be the point in finally having a child if she had to give him up? It is hard to imagine the kind of love that it took for her to make such a vow.

When the priest Eli saw Hannah agonizingly pouring her heart out to God, he thought she was out of control. He assumed she was drunk. But when he heard her desire, he asked God to grant her request. Hannah had actively put her hope in God, loving Him with trust. The Bible tells us that after that, "she went her way and ate something, and her face was no longer downcast" (1:18).

The Lord granted Hannah's request. She gave birth to a child and named him Samuel. In love again, she literally, physically gave her son to the Lord for His service, taking him to the temple and leaving him to serve with Eli.

The believers in Thessalonica understood the kind of love Hannah communicated. She faced an unjust, stressful situation, as they did centuries later. Though they were harassed and persecuted for their personal faith they didn't excuse themselves, let down, or return insults. Paul tells us that, putting their hope in God, they worked harder and loved more.

Communications that Encourage Trust

As you seek to celebrate and communicate the feminine mission, you may feel stressed and strangled. You may even question the reality of communicating love in your life. To encourage trust, we need to understand love, not as a dependent emotion but as an independent action of commitment. It is the action of love that empowers our communications that encourage trust.

Whereas the emotion of trust in love depends on the trustworthiness of another, the action of love in trust is an illustration of one's care and commitment for another. That definition of trust is not blind expectation. It is an action of boldly giving up self-satisfaction for the good of another.

Initiating Actions that Show Love

How do we initiate actions of love? First Corinthians 13 opens the window of understanding to actions that show love. Notice the thirteen qualities of love: patience, kindness, lack of envy, no boasting, not proud, not rude, not self-seeking, not easily angered, keeping no record of wrong, rejoicing in truth, trusting, hoping, and persevering. Each of those qualities relates to communications that encourage trust.

Practical Truth

Kindness. Practical truth, the discipline of speaking truth, can be initiated by kindness. The words we speak may not be erroneous, but if they are not clothed with kindness, they are not actions of love. They will be hollow and blaring, often hurting. They are compared to a "a resounding gong or a clanging cymbal."

Kind truth is controlled, not emotional. Kind truth is sensitive, not seething. Yet kind truth may also be confrontational. I show my love to my children in little ways by kindly telling them a truth that will save them embarrassment ("You have ink on your shirt") and, in more profound ways, that will save them from calamity (with verbal confrontation and restriction from immorality).

Pleasantness. It is not necessary to be rude with the truth. Rudeness is not an action of love. It seems almost too obvious to state, yet in our zeal to share the truth we are sometimes rude. At such times even though the message of truth is presented it lacks power and does not result in hope because it was not given with sensitivity or understanding.

Joy. We can both initiate and respond with joy. Rejoice and celebrate truth. Ah, joy is an emotion, is it not? Rejoicing can also be an action. We rejoice on the occasions of birthdays, anniversaries, and other special days. How? By setting aside time to remember and honor. That way rejoicing becomes an action.

Give special time to truth. Do you give attention to truth? When you speak and respond it should be with care. Worship is a time to actively rejoice in the truth. Appreciating the wonders of God's creation is a way to rejoice.

Remember the truth. Do you repeat and record what is good and pure? Doing so requires an active effort. Consider making a memory scrapbook of what is true and good. Celebrate truth by reviewing and sharing it.

Honor truth. Do you honor truth with your words and actions? Show others your esteem for the truth with your response to hearing it. Show others your esteem for truth by the care you give to speaking truth.

Persevering. Persevering at times means striving, but it is most often an action of endurance. Parents must learn the action of enduring in truth. It involves self-control, not giving up or giving in. It is an action of love.

Practical Trust

Patience. Patience is one of the practical actions of trust. "Love is patient," says Paul. The request to "be patient" because "God is not finished with me yet" is a plea for trust in love.

Not envious, not boastful, not proud. In our relationship to God those actions involve turning away from self toward Him as the object of our glory. The Thessalonians were commended for that action in Paul's first letter to them. "You became a model. . . . You turned to God from idols to serve the living and true God" (1:7, 9).

In our relationship to others that kind of trust action is a product of unselfishness. Envy is desiring more for self. Boasting is attempting to elevate self. Pride is complimenting self. Such actions seriously impair trust between people. Trust can be the action of self-control that causes you to let go of your desire for significance and seek the good of another.

Not seeking self. A loving action of trust allows others to use their gifts. Are you tempted to grumble that someone cannot be trusted because she does not do things your way? Showing respect for someone else's work, even though it may be different from or not as good as yours, will empower your relationship with that person. The Thessalonians were urged "to respect those who work hard among you, who are over you," holding "them in the highest regard in love because of their work" (1 Thessalonians 5:12–13).

Not easily angered. Trust can be a confidence that controls anger. Again, it is not an action of blind dependence on another in this sense but an action of putting hope in God rather than fuming about suspicions.

Not keeping a record of wrong. This action communicates trust by focusing on the issue of the moment rather than building up a list, mentally or literally, of offenses. It is easy to compound a problem by pulling out our lists of character flaws. You know how it goes, reciting one's errors from day one of a relationship. "Make sure that nobody pays back wrong for wrong, but always try to be kind to each other and to everyone else" (v. 15).

Trust. This is the action that allows another to take responsibility. It communicates love by giving someone else the opportunity to grow. It does not have to mean that you believe that person will be perfect, but it does mean that the experience will be for her good. As we activate this kind of love we should "be joyful always; pray continually; give thanks in all circumstances, for this is God's will for you in Christ Jesus" (v. 16).

Hope. This action of love looks to the future. "Do not put out the Spirit's fire; do not treat prophecies with contempt. Test everything. Hold on to the good. Avoid every kind of evil" (vv. 19–22).

Why? "For I know the plans I have for you," declares the Lord, "plans to prosper you and not to harm you, plans to give you hope and a future" (Jeremiah 29:11).

Increasing Actions that Show Love

Paul's second letter to the Thessalonians is an encouragement to them to increase their actions that show love.

He suggests six ways in which we can empower our communication by increasing our actions that show love: by faith, by fearlessness, by focus, by firmness, by faithfulness, and by following.

Increasing Faith

The Thessalonians continued to demonstrate their belief in the testimony of God given by Paul, Silas, and Timothy. Paul presents more evidence to them of God's plan for the future as an encouragement to their faith.

Communications that Encourage Trust

"With this in mind," he writes, "we constantly pray for you, that our God may count you worthy of his calling, and that by his power he may fulfill every good purpose of yours and every act prompted by your faith" (2 Thessalonians 1:11). You will be encouraged and increase in faith as you study God's Word, gaining knowledge of His message.

Increasing Fearlessness

The media preachers of Paul's day were alarming some of the people. Paul urged the Thessalonians to be fearless, telling them not to "become easily unsettled or alarmed by some prophecy, report or letter supposed to have come from us, saying that the day of the Lord has already come. Don't let anyone deceive you in any way" (2:2–3).

Our confidence increases as we put our hope in God, trusting the truth of His Word rather than being terrified by the possible interpretation of events that surround us.

Increasing Focus

In chapter 2, verses 5–12, we see the increasing need to keep our focus. We are not to be confused or disconcerted by wickedness as if there were no hope. This lawlessness will end. When the Lord Jesus returns, He will overthrow Satan (v. 8). Focus on the truth, the writer tells us. In the midst of wickedness, people do not perish because there is no hope. "They perish because they refused to love the truth and so be saved" (v. 10). We are to focus on the truth and love it. That is what keeps our love growing and our actions of love going when lawlessness surrounds us.

Increasing Firmness

"Stand firm and hold to the teachings we passed on to you" (2:15). The Thessalonians were known for their endurance. That is one of the reasons others were drawn to them. Isn't it true that among political and religious leadership, we watch who will endure? A new leader arises, and we watch to see if he or she lasts.

I remember an educational leader who was charismatic and qualified—the answer to everyone's dream. The problem was that he didn't stay long enough in any one place to make a difference. He worked two years in one place, one year in another. Then he went on to stay eighteen months somewhere else. He lacked endurance.

It is difficult to stand firm, to endure when the pressures of life surround us. That is why Paul said, "May our Lord Jesus Christ himself and God our Father, who loved us and by his grace gave us eternal encouragement and good hope, encourage your hearts and strengthen you in every good deed and word" (2:16-17).

Increasing Faithfulness

Faithfulness is evidence of love action. It is by the faithfulness of the Lord that we are strengthened, protected, and confident. Paul encourages, "May the Lord direct your hearts into God's love and Christ's perseverance" (3:5).

Increasing Following

Paul, Silas, and Timothy tried to live what they taught, and they urged the Thessalonians to do the same. "For you yourselves know how you ought to follow our example. We were not idle when we were with you. . . . We worked night and day, laboring and toiling so that we would not be a burden to any of you. We did this, not because we do not have the right to such help, but in order to make ourselves a model for you to follow" (3:7-9).

Their message was twofold: "Follow our leadership, and we will pay our own way, working like everyone else." The Thessalonians were doing that, but Paul wanted them to increase in those actions of love. We, too, must persevere, considering our work and labor as actions of love. Paul said, "We always thank God for all of you, mentioning you in our prayers. We continually remember before our God and Father your work produced by faith, your labor prompted by love, and your endurance inspired by hope in our Lord Jesus Christ" (1 Thessalonians 1:2–3).

As we identify, initiate, and increase actions that show love, we communicate hope to others and are empowered in our mission.

Discovering Your Mission

1. If Hannah were here today, how would you tell her to respond to "the other woman"? How would the goals of the feminine mission influence your response?
2. Read 1 Corinthians 13, looking at the descriptions of love as actions. Give an example of how one of those love actions would empower you in your mission.

Further Research

Select a women's issue, and suggest ways in which you could implement the principle of communication power by love actions to help that cause.

8

Communications that Build Dreams

*The lips of the righteous nourish many. . . .
The tongue of the wise brings healing.*

Proverbs 10:21; 12:18

The words "Mother on Strike" were neatly printed across the placard. Lee Ann propped her sign in front of the house and sat down on a plastic lawn chair with a book.

Lee Ann continued her picket protest for three days. The weekly news took her picture. We, her friends in the neighborhood Bible study, listened to her story and were mystified by her mercurial family relationship.

Lee Ann was open and eager to learn truth. How could she integrate the troubling issues of womanhood and biblical theology?

The Bible gives numerous examples of the impact of our words. The woman who communicates with personal language, purity, purpose, and thoughtful language increases her power and inspires vision and hope.

The Power of Personal Language

In real life an exchange of language is an essential ingredient in establishing a relationship. It seems obvious, yet observe the obsessions that imitate relationships: fans or groupies follow the words of the stars, but there is no personal exchange of language; a man or woman fantasizes about a possible future with another, yet the other fails to respond to communications; we speak fervent words to God about our needs and fail to listen to His personal word to us.

There must be a mutual exchange of personal language, seasoned by a spirit of respect and responsibility for an encounter to pass the stage of acquaintance and enter the phase of establishing a positive relationship.

The Power of Pure Language

The book of Proverbs speaks of the relational value of a pure heart and gracious speech. Friendships can only grow when our motives are pure. "He who loves a pure heart and whose speech is gracious will have the king for his friend" (Proverbs 22:11).

The Purpose of Respectful and Responsible Language

To Support People

Respect is a matter of consideration. Respect does not tangle with self-esteem but reaches out the hand of honor to acknowledge the esteem of another. Peter urges us to "show proper respect to everyone," and Paul asks us "to respect those who work hard" and reminds wives to respect their husbands. (1 Peter 2:17; 1 Thessalonians 5:12; Ephesians 6:22).

The Scriptures also list specific actions worthy of respect: communicating kindness, living a quiet life, working with one's hands, maintaining temperance and trustworthiness, and avoiding malicious talk (see 1 Thessalonians; 2 Timothy).

To Support Relationships

Responsibility recognizes individual identity and accountability. Responsibility means more than assigning obligation; it acknowledges ownership of and care for one's communications.

It is interesting to note that though many women express the fear that they might lose their identity in marriage, it was man who first tried to merge his identity with woman. The Genesis record states that it was Adam who blurted out his feelings of fear when God came looking for him in the Garden. Why?

"Because I was naked," he said.

Adam was wearing fig leaves by then and, of course, God already knew what had happened, but with those words Adam really blew his cover.

"Who told you that you were naked?" God asked. His question allowed Adam the opportunity to take responsibility for his actions.

"Have you eaten from the tree that I commanded you not to eat from?" Adam couldn't deny that he had eaten the fruit, but suddenly he thought it would sound better if he explained that he never would have done such a thing on his own. Everyone was doing it, you know—Eve and the serpent—and it looked like fun. It was kind of a group thing. He had been confused by peer pressure.

Eve must have decided that was a good defense because she followed the same line.

"What is this you have done?" God said.

"The serpent deceived me, and I ate," she quickly explained.

Adam and Eve merged their identities and relinquished the ownership of their actions.

God's response was not only a pronouncement of the consequences of their sin, but He included an illustration of their responsibilities. With this background, His words recorded in Genesis 3:16 may be understood, not as a curse against women, but as a clarification of responsibility. Eve would desire to control and cover for Adam, but God would hold Adam accountable.

That interpretation also clarifies the picture of biblical submission. It is not the sacrifice of individual identity. It is not one person owning another. Instead, it allows another to take responsibility and resists the pressure of yielding to the domination of another.

The Power of Thoughtful Language

As you seek to follow the feminine mission, using your distinctive gifts to inspire hope and vision, you are responsible for the powerful effect of your language choices. Words have the power to dispel anger, to cheer, to change one's countenance, to charm. The Scriptures indicate the potency of thoughtful language. Notice the way words empower: "A gentle answer turns away wrath, but a harsh word stirs up anger" (Proverbs 15:1). And, "An anxious heart weighs a man down, but a kind word cheers him up" (12:25).

What are the words that can change a countenance? Songs of the Lord. God praise. "Put your hope in God, for I will yet praise him, my Savior and my God" (Psalm 42:5). Some translations say "the help of my countenance" in place of "my Savior."

How can you express your feelings effectively? With well-chosen word pictures. "A word aptly spoken is like apples of gold in settings of silver" (Proverbs 25:11).

Understanding three language dynamics will help us to create positive dialogue: The first is the strength of the silent language of culture; the second is the power of I-you language; and the third is the endurance of word pictures.

The Power of the Silent Language of Culture

If you have ever studied a foreign language, you know that communicating in that language is far more complex than just memorizing the translation of words. I watched an American woman pay an outrageous sum for sandals to a vendor on the beach of Acapulco a few years ago. Since she understood a few words of Spanish, she apparently felt comfortable agreeing with the suggested price. What she failed to realize was that there is more to understanding language than knowing the meaning of the words or text. Though the vendor said that the cost of the sandals was thirty dollars, he didn't expect her to pay thirty dollars. She didn't know about the custom of bargaining. She was expected to make a counter offer, perhaps five dollars. The vendor would laugh and begin to walk away but would return to suggest a price of twenty dollars. She might then suggest eight, he fifteen, she ten. And they could probably make a deal for about twelve dollars. Because she did not understand the silent language of culture, she paid far more than necessary—the full thirty dollars.

The silent language of culture is strengthened by understanding the meaning of words, or the text, understanding the use of words, or the timing, and understanding the impact of words, or the thought.

Strength of Text

Lee Ann chose three words for her announcement: "Mother on Strike." The impact of her text was dependent on what those words meant individually and together.

The Celebration of Womanhood

Semantics involve our understanding or the meaning of individual words. The word strike by itself might mean one person punching another or, as intended in Lee Ann's case, a notice of refusal to work.

Syntax involves our understanding or the meaning given to a group of words and how they are arranged. If the words had been reversed to read, "Strike on Mother," they would have conveyed an entirely different meaning.

Why is it important to understand that? Sometimes well-meaning words intended as a bridge of love become barriers of contention because of blunders in syntax and semantics.

When our youngest child was born we somehow fell into the habit of calling her Baby. As a two-year-old lost at the Wonderland park in Toronto, Canada, she was asked her name. "Baby," she sweetly replied. As a teenager, she doesn't feel so sweet about the name Baby. That four-letter symbol means something different to her now. She is growing up, and Baby denotes someone less than mature in her eyes.

Scholars who study semantics investigate the history of words, what they used to mean, and how their meaning is changing.

If we wish to communicate strong, positive symbols, we need to be aware of the various meanings that individual words and the arrangement of those words may give.

Strength of Timing

There is a time for everything, and a season for every activity under heaven:

> a time to be born and a time to die,
> a time to plant and a time to uproot,
> a time to kill and a time to heal,

Communications that Build Dreams

> a time to tear down and a time to build,
> a time to weep and time to laugh,
> a time to mourn and a time to dance,
> a time to scatter stones and a time to gather them,
> a time to embrace and a time to refrain,
> a time to search and a time to give up,
> a time to keep and a time to throw away,
> a time to tear and a time to mend,
> a time to be silent and a time to speak,
> a time to love and a time to hate,
> a time for war and a time for peace.
>
> Ecclesiastes 3:1–8

The timing of words can strengthen or weaken relationships. Communication time bombs are explosive words delivered without warning.

When you are at home or at work, apart from your family or friends, do you meditate on or rehearse an emotional response to an earlier altercation? Perhaps you suspect something, and you pounce on your loved one with your words the minute you see him or her. Do you sometimes express your anger or disapproval without regard to the task your husband, child, student, or friend is trying to fulfill at the moment? Listen to where they are before you speak. Communication time bombs can devastate a relationship.

Strength of Thought

Euphemisms are pleasing words that are used to replace an harsh expression. Instead of saying that the new neighbor is pushy, you could describe her as enthusiastic.

"Why beat around the bush?" you ask. Because there are times when bluntness blocks communication.

One caution is important. Euphemisms should always be truthful and thoughtful. A lie cannot be excused as a euphemism. And meaningless, shallow expressions serve no greater purpose than the original word.

The Power of "I-you" Language

We all use "I-you" language. The term "I-you" language is simply a label that helps us identify our attitudes. "You" language assumes an authoritarian position and often puts the listener on the defensive.

"You are always late. You ruin our dinnertime. You don't care about how hard I work."

"I" language allows the listener room to receive, consider, and respond to the speaker's message. It encourages continued dialogue and growth in the relationship.

"I feel upset when you are late. I miss you when you are not here for dinner, and it makes me feel that the preparations I make for our meals are not important to you."

"I" language is particularly helpful for confrontational conversation. It encourages clear, concise, and controlled expression.

Power of Clear Expression

When someone makes you angry, it is not difficult to say, "You make me so mad"—and to stop short of explaining why a certain behavior kindled your anger. It is not enough to merely add, "You make me so mad when you came home late from work." Though you know why the late arrival offends you, that may not be clear to the other person. Framing your feelings with "I" language will add clarity to your expression.

"I am mad because I feel that you take me for granted when you are late."

"I" language has the power of clarifying uncertainties. It eliminates elusive fantasies and reveals the real issues of a relationship.

Power of Concise Expression

Once we begin a confrontation with "you" language, it is easy to continue on a "you" language roll.

"You make me mad. And you—you don't care anyway. I should have known when we first met that you were selfish. You forgot my birthday. And speaking of birthdays, you don't appreciate all the work I go to for your birthdays. How many years of birthdays has it been? You are starting to show your age. You should lose weight, you know. You need a haircut too. Oh, you never did return those library books I asked you to pick up for me. You just don't know how to shop."

How much better it would be to simply express your feelings in "I" language. "I am hurt that you forgot my birthday." That is honest without attacking. It allows the one who forgot to respond. Though using "I" language may at first seem awkward, it can prove to be a powerful tool of expression. As you pause to think about reversing "you" to "I" language, it will be easier to determine the relevant issues and express them concisely.

Power of Controlled Expression

"I" language also encourages rational and responsible expression. Statements of facts or feelings will tend to be more controlled as we consider our reasoning. At the same time we are able to evaluate the degree of responsibility that we should assume in the circumstances.

The Endurance of Word Pictures

Imagery opens the "doorways to the mind."[1] Like colors added to the pictures of communication, the language of imagery influences our perceptions of a message. Alan

Monroe divides the language of imagery into seven classes or senses: visual, auditory, gustatory, olfactory, tactual, kinesthetic, and organic.[2]

When we communicate through word pictures, we are able to affect the auditory sense, coloring the pictures that enter the doorways to the mind. An emotional word picture is "a communication tool that uses a story or object to articulate simultaneously the emotions and intellect of a person."[3]

A child once observed a drawstring purse and said to me, "I want to be in the bag."

"What do you mean?" I asked.

"You know, inside the bag it is safe and warm, and you can just close it up when you want to."

"In the bag" suddenly became a meaningful word picture. It described security, comfort, retreat, a place of refuge. That picture has often come to my mind through the years. There are moments when we all would like to be "in the bag."

Try to create word pictures to communicate your feelings in times of emotional conflict. The memory of a word picture will endure and edify a relationship long after a crisis in communication.

Communication that builds relationships will be supported by respectful and responsible language.

Learn to say:

"I like to hear your ideas."

"I enjoy you."

"I want to encourage you."

"I support you."

"I love you."

You can learn to inspire hope and vision by giving thought to your language. Your words may encourage a dream.

Discovering Your Mission

1. How does pure language inspire hope and vision?
2. Describe the characteristics of respectful and responsible language.
3. Try to recall something said to you that uniquely inspired and challenged you. In what way or how did those words make a difference?

Further Research

Read the book *Tongue in Check* by Joseph Stowell. Note both the negative and positive images of power communications.

NOTES

1. Quoted in Alan H. Monroe, *Principles and Types of Speech Communication*, 10th ed. (Glenview, Ill.: Scott, Foresman, 1986), 238. From Victor Avin Ketcham, "The Seven Doorways to the Mind," in *Business Speeches by Business Men*, ed. William P. Sandford and Hayes Yeager (New York: McGraw-Hill, 1930).
2. Ibid., 235.
3. Gary Smalley and John Trent, *The Language of Love* (Pomona, Calif.: Focus on the Family, 1988), 17.

9

Communications that Face Conflict

*N*ever tire of doing what is right.
2 Thessalonians 3:13

Carolyn couldn't erase the images of taunting, the beatings, the humiliation from her mind. Outwardly she pursued a successful career as a university professor and popular speaker. Inwardly she struggled to bury the memories of conflicts in her past.

Even her intimate friends were unaware of the real picture of her childhood. They were mystified by her occasional reaction of ready-to-punch clenched fists when they unexpectedly came behind her with a raised hand. She saw the vision of her abusive, alcoholic father raising his arm to beat her and remembered the many times she had fled from his presence or was told by both parents to "get out."

In the mesmerizing story of her search for hope and healing, Carolyn Koons wrote:

> The intense pain I felt forced me to once again sever all connections with my family. My people-filled life at Azusa [University] sometimes felt like a new family where I could grow up all over again in a home where people saw enough potential in me to put up with my immaturities and stubborn attitudes. I flourished on the outpouring of love and affirmation.

> Still, each time my parents unexpectedly broke into the present, an emotional club bludgeoned my self-esteem. When I'd picture my father, I'd see myself through his eyes and feel worthless. My memories were like quicksand—with the first horrible thought, the rest would pull me downward.
>
> My father's enraged face haunted my dreams. In recurring nightmares he chased me, brandishing that same black, loaded .38-caliber handgun. He'd come into my classroom and cry out in a frenzy, "This time I'm going to do it. I'm going to kill you." When he had me trapped against the chalkboard, he'd grin delightedly at my students, turn to point the gun at me, and squeeze off one fatal shot point blank into my head.[1]

While she was publicly instrumental in expanding the horizons of multitudes, privately Carolyn was plagued by a shrunken image of herself as a little girl whenever there was a question about her past. She shares her journey of changing visions of anger to victorious action, the day-by-day process of inner healing in the book *Beyond Betrayal*.

Like Paul, Timothy, Silas, and the Thessalonian church, Carolyn continued to suffer from abusive words and actions of opposition, preventing her from making whole connections with even her most intimate friends. How can we further the feminine mission when we are caught in the center of conflict? What is the right thing to do?

Though the counsel of Peter was specifically to women in conflict with their husbands, and the letters from Paul were written as personal advice in response to the Thessalonian problems, they speak to our needs as the inspired, living Word of God. These Scriptures reveal that our communications in conflict are empowered by attitudes as well as actions.

Empowerment of Attitudes

Women facing mental, emotional, or physical abuse, whether in the present or past, face the most difficult obstacle in pursuing the feminine mission. The attitudes that can positively influence our communications are boldness, loyalty, delight, and perseverance.

The power for the endurance of those attitudes is not naturally generated in times of difficulty, but it is "inspired by hope in our Lord Jesus Christ" (1 Thessalonians 1:3).

Boldness

"We had previously suffered and been insulted in Philippi, as you know," writes Paul, "but with the help of our God we dared to tell you his gospel in spite of strong opposition" (2:2).

God empowers us to pursue our mission in times of conflict as we put our hope in Him. When you think you must improve your circumstances, resolve difficulties, or become a better person before daring to go on, remember that you can dare because of Him—the hope that He gives and the future that He promises—not the conditions of today.

When someone under our care seems to be walking away from all that is good and true, it is easy to feel like a failure. It is not only abuse but consistently disobedient or irresponsible conduct in the lives of those we love and nurture that discourages us. Parents, a mother, teachers and counselors, pastors, and friends all suffer when we have invested our hopes in someone who ignores the path of righteousness.

I have seen the reaction of women who feel that they cannot go on. They consider themselves failures and suffer from discouragement and sometimes chronic depression.

But the key to daring is not in the momentary emotional feeling of hope or despair that we may have in another person but in the certainty of our hope in God. We dare to hold our heads high and keep on saying and doing what we know is right, knowing that it is God who will work in us (and in those we love) "to will and to act according to his good purpose" (Philippians 2:13).

Loyalty

"We are not trying to please men but God, who tests our hearts," said Paul. "We were not looking for praise from men, not from you or anyone else. As apostles of Christ we could have been a burden to you, but we were gentle among you, like a mother caring for her little children" (1 Thessalonians 2:4, 6–7).

There are two principles of devotion in spite of difficulty for us to learn. One is that God is the primary object of our devotion. When you are tempted to be discouraged because you are unappreciated, ask yourself, *Was the expectation of appreciation the reason for my devotion?*

The second principle that we see in Paul's statement is that he was devoted to the growth of individuals. He cared for the Thessalonians as a mother would care for her little children. A mother wants her children to grow—spiritually, mentally, and physically. We can persevere in times of difficulty because we are devoted to the good and growth of another.

Delight

"We loved you so much that we were delighted to share with you not only the gospel of God but our lives as well, because you had become so dear to us," Paul continued (1 Thessalonians 2:8).

Our natural inclination is not to delight in times of difficulty. We sigh and cry and groan, wondering why this is happening to us. If we have no mission but to please ourselves then suffering brings a reason for despair. It is when we put our hope in God, actively doing what we know is right in spite of our feelings, that we can focus on others and delight in them.

It is not only right to delight when times are bad, but this is the attitude that empowers our perseverance. Our delight is in God and the people He has put in our lives. We delight not because they are perfect but because He can do a perfect work in them. We delight not because we are good but because He is God.

Perseverance

"Surely you remember, brothers, our toil and hardship; we worked night and day in order not to be a burden to anyone while we preached the gospel of God to you" (1 Thessalonians 2:9).

A winning approach in perseverance is diligence. Keep on working. The Thessalonians were praised for their "labor prompted by love" (1 Thessalonians 1:3). In other references Paul reminds the people not to be idle and to confront those who are idle. He frankly calls such people busybodies. "They are not busy; they are busybodies. Such people we command and urge in the Lord Jesus Christ to settle down and earn the bread they eat" (2 Thessalonians 3:11–12).

The Power of Actions

What are we to do in times of duress? That is the question that perplexes us and perpetuates controversy. The letters to the Thessalonians clearly state four actions that empower us to persevere: controlling, conquering, encouraging, and confronting.

On Controlling

Twice in his brief first letter to the Thessalonians, Paul writes about control. In 4:3–8, he urges moral control.

> It is God's will that you should be sanctified: that you should avoid sexual immorality; that each of you should learn to control his own body in a way that is holy and honorable, not in passionate lust like the heathen, who do not know God; and that in this matter no one should wrong his brother or take advantage of him. The Lord will punish men for all such sins, as we have already told you and warned you. For God did not call us to be impure, but to live a holy life. Therefore, he who rejects this instruction does not reject man but God, who gives you his Holy Spirit.

The second occurrence is in 5:6–8: "So then, let us not be like others, who are asleep, but let us be alert and self-controlled. For those who sleep, sleep at night, and those who get drunk, get drunk at night. But since we belong to the day, let us be self-controlled, putting on faith and love as a breastplate, and the hope of salvation as a helmet."

In that second reference Paul reveals the way to effect this control. It is by faith, love, and hope that we can be protected and controlled, persevering in times of conflict.

On Conquering

The clue to conquering is given in 4:11–12: "Make it your ambition to lead a quiet life, to mind your own business and to work with your hands, just as we told you, so that your daily life may win the respect of outsiders and so that you will not be dependent on anybody."

When we are wronged we are concerned about what others will think of us. Will we lose people's respect because of false information? When we are denied the opportunity to clear our names it seems like the end. We feel we might as well give up.

Do not give up, Paul urges. It is by your daily life that you will win the respect of outsiders. Taking responsibility for our daily lives is also an action of perseverance. We do this by working hard to provide for our needs, not depending on others.

On Encouraging

Remember that the Thessalonians were people living in a spiritual and emotional war zone. In addition to encouraging them, Paul told them to encourage each other. Encouragement delivers energy to persevere in times of difficulty. Choose encouraging words and actions. Encourage others with your presence and with your prayers.

On Confronting

Paul alludes to a final action of perseverance in 2 Thessalonians 3:14–15: "If anyone does not obey our instruction in this letter, take special note of him. Do not associate with him, in order that he may feel ashamed. Yet do not regard him as an enemy, but warn him as a brother."

Patterns of Conflict

We can communicate hope in difficulty and change patterns of conflict into portraits of victory through loving confrontation. To understand that process we will consider the images of conflict, the implications of unresolved conflict, the intentions in conflict, and the individual responsibility in conflict.

The Celebration of Womanhood

Images in Conflict

The following clip bounced to my attention from the page of the morning newspaper:

> Talk Show Host Declares "War"
> with Head of Production Firm
>
> Vicki Lawrence has declared herself at war with the producer of her syndicated talk show, saying she has been treated so shabbily her future with "Vicki!" is uncertain.
>
> Lawrence, who said her physician has ordered her to rest and avoid stress, will be replaced by guest hosts for several weeks as the Group W Productions show wraps up taping in Burbank for the season. It airs weekday mornings on KCAL-TV Channel 9.
>
> "Life is too short to go on working with someone like this," Lawrence said of Derk Zimmerman, Group W president.
>
> She said Wednesday that she was suffering from colitis and heart palpitations brought on by her combative relationship with Zimmerman.
>
> His failure to respect her or her talent has put her "at war" with Zimmerman, she said, adding that it is up to her attorney and doctor whether she'll return to the show.[2]

The intense, warlike metaphor is a common image in conflict. We talk about attacking, defending, and shooting down arguments. Now every time Vicki Lawrence thinks of her show she replays the tapes of war images that run through her mind. With that vision, she gears herself up to fight a battle.

It is difficult to erase such images because they are embedded deep in our psyche. The picture that pops into your mind when you are in conflict propels your communications.

Professors Hocker and Wilmot, of the University of Montana, wrote of the negative images that limit the resolution of conflict and the positive images or metaphors that help to instill hope in conflict.[3] Negative images include the following ideas.

Conflict is war—"I demolished his argument."
Conflict is explosive—"Larry's got a short fuse."
Conflict is a trial—"The jury's still out on that one."
Conflict is an upward struggle—using words such as "rising power."
Conflict is a mess—"Things are falling apart down here."
Conflict is a game—"Toss the ball into his court."
Conflict is a heroic adventure—using words such as "bigger and better."

Can there be such a thing as "productive conflict"? Hocker and Wilmot noted that "the relationship that moves through episodes of conflict will grow, change, and be altered in important ways."[4] The positive results of productive conflict are many. The researchers describe five "good things."

- Each person feels a greater sense of "zest" (vitality, energy).
- Each person feels more able to act and does act productively.
- Each person has a more accurate picture of her/himself and the other persons(s).
- Each person feels a greater sense of worth.
- Each person feels more connected to the other persons and a greater motivation for connections with other people beyond those in the specific relationship.[5]

Creative images or word pictures can also be used to change conflict into collaborative endeavors. For instance, some suggestions include viewing conflict as a bargaining table, as a dance, or as a tide.

It is the positive images that allow productive struggles, according to Hocker and Wilmot. "And, from productive struggles emerges a new vision of humans healing their differences and working cooperatively."[6]

Implications of Unresolved Conflict

Forgiveness was announced as the next subject of discussion for our adult Sunday school class. We were new to the church, and I expected that the topic would be thoroughly explored in one Sunday or two. We would be told to forgive and forget. The discussion would probably be tedious and tense.

Instead, a husband and wife team led a dynamic, interactive study, with depth and sensitivity that exceeded anything we had ever experienced. With great wisdom and skill they probed to the core of the emotional and theological issues. The class was overflowing. We ran out of chairs. We learned that the issues of unresolved conflict are much more complex than merely programming oneself to forgive and forget.

The implications of unresolved conflict cluster in the corners of our lives and like cobwebs begin to catch the bugs of bitterness, aloofness, agitation, anger, and stereotyping.

The bugs of bitterness. Family feuds are usually based on secondhand conflicts that become entangled in a web of emotion and confusion about the facts. The resulting image of pain surfaces every time certain names are mentioned. Growing deeper than a memory, the pain pierces the chest and palpitates the heart, pushing our tongues to mumble

Communications that Face Conflict

and grumble long after the original conflict. The bugs of bitterness cannot be buried. Unless they are completely removed they continue to propagate, eroding not only your relationships but others also.

The writer of Hebrews likens those bugs to a root and warns: "See to it that no one misses the grace of God and that no bitter root grows up to cause trouble and defile many" (Hebrews 12:15). And James continues, "But if you harbor bitter envy and selfish ambition in your hearts, do not boast about it or deny the truth. . . . For where you have envy and selfish ambition, there you find disorder and every evil practice" (James 3:14, 16).

The bugs of aloofness. We learn to play it safe when we've been hurt. Why should you give when you've learned that you get nothing back? Why risk a verbal or physical beating? The bug of aloofness seems like a friendly bug at first. Like a nonlethal spider, it eats other more distasteful bugs. It is protective. But it multiplies. Soon the bugs of aloofness distance you further and further from personal relationships. The friendly insulation of the bugs of aloofness begins to surround you until you are left in lonely isolation.

That is one reason we are urged to "make every effort to live in peace with all men and to be holy" (Hebrews 12:14).

The bugs of agitation. Time does not dissolve conflict. Issues that are left unattended invite the bugs of agitation. Even when you have consciously forgotten an incident, your hidden memory tape may be stimulated by a sound, a voice, or a season—causing nervous tension, weeping, abruptness, and renewed conflict. The bugs of agitation must be eliminated before they weigh you down, sinking you into chronic depression.

The bugs of anger. The bugs of anger are energetic creatures, striking out their poisoned fangs in every direction. "Let it all out," we are encouraged. "It's therapeutic."

But the bugs of anger do not die of exhaustion. If they are not fully exterminated, they smolder and renew themselves in the night. For that reason we are advised, "Do not let the sun go down while you are still angry" (Ephesians 4:26).

The bugs of stereotyping. Carolyn Koons said it was difficult for her to relate to others' acceptance of her, especially in family situations, during the years she buried the facts and her feelings about her father. She tells of a particularly loving family that decided to "adopt" her as an adult. "Come on, you can call us Mom and Dad," they cajoled. She could not do so, because "Mom" and "Dad" were negative images to her. Because of the deep unresolved conflict within her, she had stereotyped all mom and dad pictures. They all looked alike to her.

The bugs of stereotyping grew and infected her relationships with other men and women who reached out as extended family to her. For years she was afraid to risk talking about her past for fear of repeated rejection.

Every time she thought she had buried the bugs of bitterness, aloofness, aggravation, anger, and stereotyping by ignoring her past, they crawled back across her face. She'd brush them aside, and they would reappear. In the moving story of the process of her inner healing, Carolyn Koons relates how she finally eliminated the "bugs" and how she learned to communicate hope to other hurting people in conflict.

Intentions in Conflict

What are your goals in confronting conflict? To put the other person in her place? To squash perceived rebellion or to verify your authority?

Emotional reactions can lunge from within and burst out so rapidly that we are astounded by the fervor of our feelings. We justify our reactions by measuring the injustice of others. They were wrong. Pride and selfish ambition motivate such reactions.

The Christians who lived in the northern part of Asia Minor were being persecuted for their faith. It was unfair. They were clearly doing what was right. The world around them was clearly living a pagan existence. Jesus' disciple Peter wrote a letter to the Christians, urging them to control their reactions and to think of the greater goal in confronting the opposition.

"Prepare your minds for action; be self-controlled," he wrote, and "set your hope fully on the grace to be given you when Jesus Christ is revealed" (1 Peter 1:13). In other words, think ahead about the best action in confronting conflict. Control the emotions that jump up in your throat. How can we do that? We begin by setting our hope in God.

Peter repeats a similar message throughout his letter, stipulating even more specific actions. "Do not repay evil with evil or insult with insult. . . . For, 'Whoever would love life and see good days must keep his tongue from evil and his lips from deceitful speech. He must turn from evil and do good; he must seek peace and pursue it'" (1 Peter 3:9-11). Our intentions in confronting conflict should be to seek peace (resolution) and to do good for another.

Carolyn Koons writes about her adopted son Tony's adjustment to a new culture, a new language, and a new school. He was abandoned at the age of five and lived for seven years in a Mexican prison because no one knew where else to put him. There were inevitable conflicts in his new world.

One teacher in particular was rankled by Tony's behavior. The teacher was furious when he ordered the class to copy a sentence from the blackboard and Tony failed to comply. The teacher's chief concern was to maintain his authority, and that was justified. But it should not have overshadowed or replaced the intention of seeking resolution in the conflict and doing good for Tony.

Is your chief concern to prove another wrong? Do you pridefully maintain (since you are right) that the other must come to you and ask forgiveness? Has your righteousness become a barrier to doing good and pursuing peace? What is your responsibility?

Individual Responsibility in Conflict

We can communicate hope in conflict, changing visions of anger to victorious action by developing a clear picture of facts and feelings. That is our responsibility. We can take steps to resolve conflict.

Specify points of conflict. In this step, through words or images, identify the facts and feelings involved in the conflict. It is important to do this privately so that you can think more clearly. Write down, doodle, or draw pictures of the incident, identifying how you feel about it, and how you think the other party feels.

Sometimes this practical process softens and simplifies the issues to the extent that you can decide whether there is an actual conflict or a need for clarification of communication.

Picture possible resolutions. This is the step in which you visualize the outcome of the conflict. Three directions are possible. You could end up in a win-lose situation, a lose-lose situation, or a win-win situation.

In a win-lose situation one party clearly comes out on top and the other on the bottom. This is the situation of the bulls and bullfighters in Spain. It is a fight to the death. The fight isn't over until one definitely wins and the other loses. It is almost always the bull who loses.

In a lose-lose situation it is hardly worth fighting. Both parties will be so badly damaged by insistence on their way that they lose more than they had in the first place.

Win-win is the ideal result of confrontation in conflict. Both parties may give a little, but each will gain something as well. How can we create a win-win situation? The way in which we communicate our concerns can make all the difference.

Enlarge the picture. It is time to look at the big picture and consider how to confront our conflict. Again, before taking action, it is wise to literally visualize this enlargement. Your options are to pull back, push forward, passively persist, hold hostility, or assertively communicate.

When it actually comes to the confrontation, a surprising number of people are intimidated by the risk, and they decide to do nothing or pull back. Their lack of expression does not make the conflict go away. It merely submerges the reality of the relationship, limiting it to superficial exchanges. That is what happens when you decide that a situation is lose-lose. Believing that there is no resolution, you continue a relationship with role-play.

On the other hand, direct aggressive action is usually an uncontrolled response. Rather than resolving the conflict it further exacerbates the issues.

Though the media flings out fictional scenarios of friends shouting phrases such as, "Get out of my house!" or, "I never want to see you again; I'll kill you!" and minutes later repenting and lovingly remembering all that they mean to each other, that is rarely how it works in real life. Direct aggressive action is always damaging.

Whereas direct aggression is obvious, we are often oblivious to passive aggression. Passive aggressive action is the unsaid barb you read between the lines, the absence of support that used to be there, the intonation that leaves you unsure of its meaning. Sarcasm is one example of passive aggression.

Withholding your heart is similar to passive aggression, though not hostile. Though indirect communication withholds mean messages, it still hurts. It is noted more by lack of communication than by definitive actions.

Assertiveness is not a bad word. "Assertiveness is important to growth," writes Christian psychologist Stanley Lindquist.[7] Assertive action is clear, concise, and straightforward. That is what Jesus recommended to His disciples.

> If your brother sins against you, go and show him his fault, just between the two of you. If he listens to you, you have won your brother over. But if he will not listen, take one or two others along, so that every matter may be established by the testimony of two or three witnesses. If he refuses to listen to them, tell it to the church; and if he refuses to listen even to the church, treat him as you would a pagan or a tax collector. (Matthew 18:15–17)

Projecting a new image. You must carefully plan how you will create a new picture. Plan to use words that nourish relationships, create word pictures, be willing to linger a while and listen to the other party, look for ways to show God's love and build trust.

When you follow these steps, preparing your mind for action, controlling your emotions, and putting your hope in God, you will triumph in doing right without fear.

Discovering Your Mission

1. What fears keep you from doing the right thing and facing conflict?
2. Discuss the application of 1 Thessalonians 4:11–12 to a current women's issue.

Further Research

Review *Pressure Points,* by Gary Oliver and H. Norman Wright, and summarize how the central themes correlate with the goal of doing right without fear.

NOTES

1. Carolyn Koons, *Beyond Betrayal: Healing My Broken Past* (San Francisco: Harper & Row, 1986), 204.
2. The Associated Press, May 27, 1993.
3. Joyce L. Hocker and William W. Wilmot, *Interpersonal Conflict,* 3d ed. (Dubuque, Iowa: Brown and Benchmark, 1991), 25–29.
4. Ibid., 37.
5. Ibid., 38–39.
6. Ibid., 43.
7. Stanley E. Lindquist, *Reach Out . . . Become an Encourager* (Wheaton, Ill.: Creation House, 1983), 135.

Part Three

CONFIRMATION POWER

The Principle of Confirmation Power

As you confirm the reality of your eternal purpose in the home environment, leadership, the workplace, friendships, and in diverse communities, you will be empowered to celebrate the feminine mission.

The Contemporary Models of Confirmation Power

Women of our time, such as Glenna, Beth, Sue, and Sally, reaching out beyond themselves, daring to confirm their mission, demonstrate the reality of God's power in our everyday lives.

10

Confirming Purpose in the Home

The wise woman builds her house, but with her own hands the foolish one tears hers down.

Proverbs 14:1

Homeless shelters offer room and board. In Minneapolis, accommodations at The Drake include an opportunity to work for pocket change, free newspapers, free telephone calls for jobs, and a bag lunch and bus fare when you go to a job. Dwight Hobbes called it "a soft landing shelter."[1] Though some found it so good that they were reluctant to leave, it wasn't really home. There were soft beds, warm meals, televisions, radios, and people. Just what was missing that makes a place a home? Like a hotel, it was not only temporary; it was of necessity a generic dwelling place that provided for minimum needs. It lacked the environment of a real home.

Though we may joke about a bachelor's apartment needing "a woman's touch," it is true that women instinctively create a change in environment. I am not speaking of cooking, housekeeping, and decorating, though women who are gifted in those areas make a great contribution to a home. "A woman's touch" is an influence that is deeper and perhaps less deliberate than those gifts. It is the effect she creates in the environment as a result of who she is and how she desires to relate to others.

The Celebration of Womanhood

A woman, whether married or single, is the environmental master of her home. She influences her surroundings by creating an atmosphere, attitudes, alternatives, and advantages.

Creating an Atmosphere

Beth's place is not very big, and she hasn't had time to accumulate great riches since college and graduate school, but she has a real home. She lives alone with her cat, Kelsey, but her little apartment is not a lonely place. When you stop by you feel a warmth. It is easy to linger, and the atmosphere is inviting. Is it the furnishings? Is it the smell of a roast in her oven?

No, there is something more. It is Beth herself—who she is and how she relates to others. People are drawn to her home because she creates an atmosphere of hospitality and refuge.

The Heart of Hospitality

"I can't have people over because my place is too small."

"We haven't finished redecorating."

"You see, I live alone, so it's difficult for me to have people over."

"Our family is so big. It's difficult enough to feed them."

"I've invited lots of people over, and they don't invite me back so I'm quitting."

Those are true responses of women who have been encouraged to open their homes to others. They have misunderstood the heart of hospitality. We hear the message of the New Testament that urges us to show hospitality, practice hospitality, and offer hospitality, but what does it mean?

Biblical hospitality means opening your heart as you open your home. If you have ever visited or stayed with someone who showed all the signs of hospitality, the words of welcome, the meal—the works—but silently sent a message of reserve or hostility, you realize the importance of an open heart with an open home. The heart of hospitality is revealed in doing good for the guest, not seeking glory for the home.

The Refreshment of Refuge

When you show hospitality with an open heart, you create a place of refuge. A refuge is a place that is secure and safe, a place where one can escape the judgment of others and be refreshed by the affirmation of friendship. A home should be a place of refuge for your family as well as your friends.

A refuge for family. A woman can make the difference. Whether she is working outside or in the home, whether she is married or single, she is the key to the atmosphere in her home. When we are tired or pressured, it is easy to resent such unrequested power. But time and time again I have both observed and experienced that phenomenon. The mood of the woman in the home is reflected by the members of her family.

"A female distinctive through the ages has been the ability to intensify or diminish, direct or redirect the moods of others. I cannot explain it, but I am aware that women have the subtle persuasiveness when it comes to mood setting. They have 'leverage' that can move others to higher- or lower-ground,"[2] wrote Gail MacDonald.

Dr. Diane Langberg, in the book *Feeling Good, Feeling Bad*, acknowledges the reality of the problems and pain that affect the moods of many women, focusing on a woman and her body, a woman and her marriage, a woman and her family, a woman and her psychology, and a woman and her emotions. She speaks to practical questions: I love my baby, so why am I depressed? My husband is abusive—what should I do? Should I work outside the home? What is codependency? And, should I feel so guilty?[3]

Our family will be the first to see through a false facade of a happy mood. It is important to face the reality of our feelings and deal with the issues that affect our spirit.

Create a time and place for exploring and expressing troubled feelings. You may do that through a journal, by talking with a small group of trusted women or a counselor, or in the privacy of your own personal time with God. Wherever your place may be, discipline yourself to keep your exploration and expression of your troubled feelings there. It is difficult, I know, but by dragging them into the family atmosphere you invite environmental disaster.

The family's emotional response to a woman's mood is much like a chemical reaction: Her mood tends to either pollute or purify the atmosphere. A polluted home atmosphere is filled with tension, judgment, pressure for perfection, and performance beyond ability. A purified home atmosphere is filled with acceptance, affirmations, affection, and fun.

Fun? Yes. What better way to make your home a refuge than to create an atmosphere of joy. If your home is all work and no play, your family will find its fun elsewhere.

A refuge for friends. Watch the homes where people naturally congregate. Watch the women of those homes. How do they affect the atmosphere?

We first met Mel and Glenna when Mel became the pastor of our church in Michigan. Their home was always a refuge for us. Whatever they had they shared. Whoever came they heard. Today they live not far from us in southern California, and their home continues to be a place of joy and refreshment.

Why do we feel such a refuge and revitalization with them? First, they express sincere delight in our presence. They are glad to see us. Second, they are never unprepared for our presence. I am referring to the attitude they project. Of course, most gatherings are scheduled and planned, but even spontaneous visits are never marred by unspoken anxiety about more pressing matters. Third, they are open and personal, willing to share their dreams and hear ours. Fourth, they are always growing and stimulating us to grow. Fifth, they are creative and fun, willing to be both sophisticated and silly.

Even if a man in the home resists creating an open home for your friends, allow it to be a refuge for him. Consider the needs of your own family for privacy and refuge. A revolving door is not the same as being hospitable and comfortable. It is a sensitive heart and a genuine concern to do good for your family and friends that transforms a house into a home.

Creating an Attitude

It is painful to hear the frustration in the voice of a person who hates to go home. Not just children, but adults, too, often avoid the end of the day. The atmosphere is welcoming and eager, but they sense an attitude that drives them away. It's an attitude that whispers, "Come home and face up." Or, "Come home and I'll fix it. Follow my way." It can be both frightening and stifling. You can make a difference in your home by creating an attitude of growth and giving.

Let Them Grow

We may eagerly devour books about physical, intellectual, and spiritual growth, but in the process of sharing our knowledge we often stymie the growth of those around us.

The Celebration of Womanhood

With sincere and prayerful zeal we shuttle our family through progress charts, measuring ourselves against them. When our child or spouse, sister or brother fails to jump through the right hoop, we may feel personally dismayed, depressed, or angry.

Sometimes, we lovingly choke the life out of our loved ones. A responsible woman learns to nurture without smothering. She learns to let go without neglecting. It is not an easy task, because there are no set rules. The needs of each family member are unique and ever-changing. There are three questions you must ask if you wish to create an attitude of growth: Do I allow mistakes? Do I ask questions? Do I affirm progress?

Allowing mistakes. There is a great deal of difference between a deliberate, intentional wrong or failure and a mistake. Many children and teenagers are never allowed to make a mistake because they are so rigidly programmed and consistently corrected that they have never been able to experience the intellectual and spiritual exercise of making a judgment.

You can help your family members grow (even spouses and siblings) by encouraging them to consider, weigh options, search for wisdom, and make a decision. Always be ready to support, but instead of shielding them, let them learn from their mistakes. If you say, "I could have told you," you will kill the opportunity for growth.

Do you allow mistakes? It is much easier to jump in with the right answer, especially when you know you are right. Although a deliberate wrong should not be overlooked, mistakes should not be viewed as the measure of one's worth.

Asking questions. A second way to create an attitude of growth is by asking questions. Think about saying:

"What is your idea? I'd like to hear what you think."

"How would you solve this problem?"

"What do your friends say about this?"

Those questions are not for children only. Ask adults. By taking another's thoughts for granted—"Oh, I know her so well; I know what she thinks"—we stifle growth.

Affirming progress. It is embarrassing to admit. I looked at the report card, and the "C" jumped out from the page. It was the first thing I mentioned. "What happened? Why a 'C'?" There were five "A's" on the report, but my first reaction was to catch the weakness rather than affirm the progress.

A woman has a unique opportunity to encourage growth by affirming her family and friends. I am not referring to displaying the bumper sticker "I am the proud parent of an honor roll student at Clement Junior High." My children classify such signs as parental boasting rather than child boosting. "Are those parents proud of the child who isn't on the honor roll too?" they ask. Although boasting takes credit, affirmation congratulates the achievement of another. Boasting leaves little room for mistakes. Affirmation expands vision and encourages growth.

Let Them Go

We can encourage an attitude of giving by promoting—giving opportunities, giving space, and giving of ourselves.

Giving opportunities. The concept of the teachable moment may apply to teens and adults as well as children. Those moments elude us if we do not capture them spontaneously. It is the moment when someone is receptive to listen, see, and understand. When such moments do not fit into our schedule it is easy to overlook them.

Even seeming disasters can be turned into opportunities. My mother had a wonderful way of creating good in the midst of bad. When a situation seemed calamitous, she

The Celebration of Womanhood

would announce: "We're having an 'A.'" We all knew that "A" was the secret code for "adventure." It was the signal to relax, learn from the moment, and pull together. Some of our greatest memories are of our family "A's." A woman can give opportunities to her family and friends by creating a change in attitude.

Giving space. A refuge is a place apart, a place where we can separate ourselves from the rush and pressure of normal responsibilities. A woman usually controls the physical and mental space in a home. Even if your home is small, is there some place that each one can call his or her own? If it is not a private room, is there a bed, a chair, or a corner of the yard that someone might claim as his or her own space? Each of us needs a place of refuge. You are giving a gift to another by creating such a place.

Mental space is also important to consider. You can give the gift by creating private pockets of time for people. If we schedule or call people to be accountable for every minute of the day, such private pockets of time are never found.

Giving yourself. The most difficult gift is to give of ourselves. I have always loved being a mother. The shock for me—when I had my first baby at thirty-two—was not in caring, loving, or including our daughter in our lives. It was in giving of myself, my time, beyond the schedule. People, especially babies, are unpredictable. I planned schedules and creative programs and included in them my own interests of teaching Bible studies, writing, and painting. At first, I found myself feeling frustrated and worthless when the baby intruded on the accomplishment of those things. "What am I doing for society?" I asked my husband. But one of the most precious gifts we can give to another—child or adult—is ourselves. Giving up oneself may mean giving up the ambition of the moment, giving un-

Confirming Purpose in the Home

planned time, giving time at the moment needed, delaying even necessary tasks. As we model such giving, we create an attitude of giving in our home.

Creating Alternatives

As you learn to give you will learn to create alternatives. In an amazing way, a woman prepares the way for new possibilities. If your ideal for those in your home is not being met, you can complacently despair, dogmatically complain, or creatively prepare alternatives. Two key areas in which we can create alternatives are in leading and learning.

Leading

What are the alternatives when the "ideal family" as portrayed in the old first-grade reader—mother, father, two kids, and a dog named Spot—is not the picture of your family? Maybe there is a mother and father, but they are both working to make ends meet, and neither one feels like leading the family. Just who is responsible to lead?

In fact, few families fit the ideal. A woman who is willing to accept that has the opportunity to create alternatives. She can offer alternatives with spiritual leadership, social leadership, and emotional leadership.

Spiritual leadership. "My husband is not taking the spiritual leadership that I wish he would," my friend confided.

She was so bitter that she privately spoke of her doubts about her marriage. "Maybe I should have married another man. I've thought about what life would have been like," she continued.

What had happened? Was her husband such a laggard? They were both extremely active in the local church. She seemed willing to talk, so I tried to probe a little more. He was open and growing, she answered. "But he is not leading at home," she grumbled again.

"What is it that he doesn't do?"

"He doesn't read the Bible to our children at night."

To my friend, that was the sign of spiritual leadership. Did he object to her reading the Bible to the kids? No. He encouraged her.

After that day I began to listen more closely to women who complained about carrying all of the spiritual leadership. Basically, I heard them say that they had to schedule the program for spiritual family growth, and they equated that planning with spiritual leadership.

I observed families where the male figure was the one making the schedule. Were they more spiritual? Though my survey was informal, I couldn't see a correlation. In some instances, I saw men going through all the "right" motions but failing to model the fruits of the Spirit.

My friend was concerned that her husband was not speaking the language of leadership. She did not realize that spiritual leadership has little to do with lecturing and everything to do with living. The fruits of the Spirit—love, joy, peace, patience, kindness, goodness, faithfulness, gentleness, and self-control—are the true signs of spiritual leadership.

Spiritual leadership is not a role; it is the revelation of our relationship with Christ. It is the overflow of love, joy, and peace that guides those around us to the path of righteousness.

My friend was reading the wrong signs. She thought that she and her children would not grow until her husband did certain things. If she had been looking at the right signs she would have realized that she, too, was responsible for spiritual leadership, for allowing the love of God to demonstrate the fruits of the Spirit through her.

What a burden is lifted when we realize that. Yes, if there is a man in the home, he is responsible to demonstrate

Confirming Purpose in the Home

spiritual leadership. However, his leadership depends on his relationship with the Lord, and only he can do anything about that. A woman's pushing, prodding, or programming will not make him spiritual. In fact, her judgment will defeat her own spiritual leadership. A woman is equally responsible for spiritual leadership in the home.

In her overflow of love, joy, and peace, a woman can create alternatives for leading her family in spiritual growth. First, as she looks to God for daily fellowship and guidance, she can share that relationship with the family. Her leadership is thus changed from a lecture on how everyone else should live to a revelation of how she lives. Second, she looks for creative ways to teach spiritual knowledge and truth. Numerous books, music, and games are available. Be careful not to label a child as unspiritual because he or she does not like to read the Bible. Maybe reading is difficult for that child—or adult. Or perhaps his or her schooling or job involves heavy reading, and more reading is not appealing. Find what works for your family. We grow through knowledge and experience.

A third way in which a woman can provide spiritual leadership is by making room for adjustable family time. If you have a two-parent family, ask your husband how much and what time he could give to specific family time for spiritual learning. If you believe that it is important to have a routine with your children every day and you have no husband or he is not available, there is no reason you cannot lead the routine without him. Sharing in spiritual learning with the entire family is wonderful, but it is not the only way. Be sensitive to meeting the needs of each family member, not just your own need to feel you have carried out your duty. If children are older than elementary school age, include them in the discussion regarding the best time for family spiritual learning.

The Celebration of Womanhood

Social leadership. A family usually learns to let the woman lead the social schedule. Social leadership does not depend on your financial status. The keys to social leadership are caring and celebrating.

When you care about family and friends you will naturally reach out and include them in your home. Your family will usually follow your lead and do the same. If one member of the family seems to resist, you can modify your plans, still including others while respecting that individual's privacy.

Another way you can influence family social life is by making celebrations. Our family loves to celebrate. On birthdays, the most important thing to celebrate is the person. Material things are not the important part of the occasion. It is the expression of what that person means to others that counts. We sometimes assemble a collection of pictures, choosing one for each year of the person's life. It is a great time to remember experiences together. The greatest gift is to give our time and total attention to the one we celebrate.

Emotional leadership. We are sometimes the least prepared but most depended on for emotional leadership. We must think about whether we are reactive or proactive in this area. If we wait until each emotion in the family arises and then respond as we feel at the time, family members will develop a sense of insecurity, a wait-and-see-what-mood-Mom's-in stance. Whatever the situation or stress, if we think ahead, alone or with another adult, we can create reasonable alternatives. If a problem is overwhelming, instead of refusing to talk or risking hurtful talk, respond positively with a promise to talk at an agreed upon time.

Learning

A woman can also facilitate her family's growth by supplementing education and supplying education.

Confirming Purpose in the Home

Supplementing education. Awareness is the key to facilitate growth in learning. Discussing what we see around us as we travel, even to the other side of town, can stimulate growth. Respect your children's questions. Answer them or follow up later with more information.

Expose your family to new experiences, sensing a match of their talents to music, art, and athletics and encouraging them to develop in those areas.

Supplying education. A woman's involvement in the structured learning environment furthers a family's growth in learning. In both the public and private system, it is important to know who is influencing your child. Be involved. Encourage and support teachers and programs you like, rather than only getting involved when you don't like something.

If the local situation is not filling the needs of your family, you can supply your own program through home schooling. It is a good alternative for some people at some times. If you choose to do that, be sensitive to the changing needs of your children and your own needs.

Creating Advantages

Because a woman creates an atmosphere, an attitude, and alternatives, she can create advantages in the home. She can determine family benefits and personal benefits.

The family can benefit from the physical, psychological, and philosophical environment you determine.

Physical Environment

Families are not naturally clean. Most likely it was your mother who taught you to wash your hands. A woman has a great deal to do with the control of the physical environment in the home. Cleanliness and conservation are learned in the home. A woman who considers the health and nutrition of her family creates an advantage for them. A woman who encourages her family to care for the environment affirms life and preserves the beauty of God's creation for them.

Psychological Environment

When we give family members a sense of ownership, they believe home is a place where they belong. One way to do that is by designating areas of responsibility. Children share in jobs because they are part of the family home. We can also encourage belonging by designating areas of privacy.

Philosophical Environment

We have the opportunity to institute meaningful dialogue and a moral dogma in the home. Encourage peaceful negotiations among family members. You may do so by demonstrating the technique yourself the next time there is conflict. Stress a moral standard for your home.

The Feminine Mission

The woman who seeks to complete and complement the creation will be sensitive to the words of the Creator about the home. The following scriptures indicate the significance of the place called home: Genesis 43–45, a place of privacy, a place of reunion, a place of personal revelation; Exodus 9, a place of shelter; Joshua 2, a place of sanctuary; John 19, a place for family; Acts 21, 1 Corinthians 11, a place to return to, a place of physical restoration and nourishment; 1 Corinthians 14, a place of learning; 1 Timothy 5, a place of growth; Titus 2, a place of occupation; Luke 15, a place for entertainment; 2 Corinthians 5, a place in this present life.

Discovering Your Mission

1. How do you control the environment of your home? Do you create the atmosphere or do others? Why?
2. How can you advance the goals of the feminine mission in your home?

Further Research

Take a mini survey of five to ten people about the influence of their homes. Ask them how the women of their home or other people have influenced their attitudes and opportunities. Evaluate and comment on their responses as they relate to the feminine mission.

NOTES

1. Dwight Hobbes, "Wrong Way to Help the Homeless," *Reader's Digest* 142, no. 853 (May 1993), 139.
2. Gail MacDonald, *Keep Climbing* (Wheaton, Ill.: Tyndale, 1989), 41.
3. Diane Langberg, *Feeling Good, Feeling Bad* (Ann Arbor, Mich.: Servant, 1991).

11

Confirming Intentions in Leadership

*Remember your leaders, who spoke the word of
God to you.
Consider the outcome of their way of life and
imitate their faith.*

Hebrews 13:7

It was a Christmas card that triggered Elizabeth Baker's emotions about leadership—"just an ordinary Christmas card."[1]

A common old-fashioned scene adorned the card—snow, a Victorian house, and inside the window a view of a happy family celebrating the season. The father sat reading in a wing-backed chair. The mother and children gazed at him expectantly. What was it about that that made Elizabeth Baker so sad?

In *Wanting to Lead, Forced to Follow*, she explains, "The card was a clear picture of the one thing I wanted most in life—the one thing I felt I had never really been able to touch. It was a home with a godly father leading his family and making them secure in his love and provision. . . . When I looked at the card, I felt as though I were standing outside that window with my feet in the snow and my face pressed against the cold glass."[2]

A picture of leadership made her feel alone because she experienced it as a result of loss. Our feelings about leadership clearly affect the way we identify with it. If you could

The Celebration of Womanhood

create a picture postcard of a woman in leadership, what would it look like? Would she be wearing a suit, pounding a gavel, carrying a briefcase? Would your sketch include a smile, a smirk, or a sigh? Whatever your picture of a woman in leadership do you see her born as a leader, displaying traces of her current character even in childhood? Or do you think that she bargained for leadership, buying clothes and campaigns, striving for control?

Knowing a woman's intention in leadership may change our picture of her. A woman with pure intentions is seen as a servant of the people. A woman with selfish ambition may be viewed as a suppressor. Her intentions are the key to effective and enduring leadership. Consider the intentions in leadership, the conduct of leadership, and joy of leadership.

The Intentions in Leadership

What are the reasons for leadership, and why are women in leadership?

In the late 1970s, after the Watergate scandal, my husband I were sponsors for the collegiate group in our church. We were astounded at the impact of failed national leadership on the students. They were all willing to devote energy and time to the activities of the group, but no one wanted to take responsibility for leadership. We urged them to elect class officers. They were bright, creative, capable students, but they shuffled their feet and explained that it would be embarrassing to be the president. If a person wanted to be the leader, his or her intentions were suspect.

We thought they were overreacting to the request for simple responsibility. Leadership brings order to chaos, knowledge and vision to the innocent and ignorant, and energy where there is apathy. But the students were not questioning the responsibilities of leadership; each one was

Confirming Intentions in Leadership

willing to work. They finally chose two equally responsible co-presidents, thus avoiding the need to deal with the real issues that troubled them about leadership.

In the public arena, where multiple opinions clash about women's issues, theologians and lay people alike focus on issues related to leadership, often avoiding the core problem of intention. Why do we continue to quibble about qualifications, confuse equality with conquest, and prolong the tiff about titles?

The Quibble About Qualifications

The temptation is to create a "should" and "should not" list for women in leadership. Should a woman be president? Should a woman be chosen as CEO? Should a woman be a pastor?

Generic qualification or disqualification of the feminine gender is insensitive and insulting. It invalidates individual identity and intentions. The policy of affirmative action was an attempt to eliminate disqualification by color. Women added their voices to the cry for affirmation. It became an effort to eliminate unfair disqualification by gender.

What are the qualifications for productive leadership? Leadership requires the capacity to function as a guide, to gather a group, and to grow as you go. Leadership, therefore, depends entirely upon an individual's identity and intentions. It is unrelated to gender.

"God's image is man, male and female, created equals, to be in perfect harmony with one another and with their Creator. Man and woman were to function as His representatives on earth. They were to share equally in everything: in obedience, in blessings, in ruling and subduing, in reproducing, and in fellowship with God in the garden," writes Vicki Kraft.[3]

Women were created with the capacity to guide equally with men. It is a woman's individual identity, her experience and knowledge, that qualifies her to show the way in specific situations.

Can a woman communicate the way? To be a leader one must have followers. She must be able to gather a group. John V. Gilmore said, "Leadership . . . is a reciprocal relationship: one is a leader only if he is followed. Hence, for the group to be productive, the leader must meet the needs of its members."[4] That definition implies that true leadership not only shows the way but serves those who follow.

Finally, if a leader is to show and serve, she must grow as she guides. A leader who fails to grow will soon reach a level of incompetence.

Those three qualities of identity in leadership must be correlated with an assessment of one's intentions. A man or woman may be qualified by identity to be a president, a CEO, or a minister but may be an inappropriate choice for leadership in one of those positions because of his or her intentions. A woman who is focused on following the feminine mission will not fail by intention to qualify for leadership.

The Scriptures talk about this in 1 Corinthians 12 and 13. Each one is encouraged to assert his or her identity, to use his or her own unique gifts. We are to value individuality in ourselves and in others. Using the analogy of the body, Paul says, "The eye cannot say to the hand, 'I don't need you!' And the head cannot say to the feet, 'I don't need you!' On the contrary, those parts of the body that seem to be weaker are indispensable, and the parts that we think are less honorable we treat with special honor" (12:21–23).

Although we do not need to neglect our identity, the focus of effective leadership is not on the gifts of the leader but on the good of the group. The intention of true leadership is not to seek self, not to boast, not to pridefully push, but to protect, trust, and preserve.

The Confusion of Equality with Conquest

Egalitarianism is the belief in equal rights for all human beings. It is fairness and justice for all. Women in leadership sometimes confuse the concept of egalitarianism with control and conquest.

The history of feminism substantiates the problem of this confusion. Women, justifiably concerned about critical issues such as harassment, discrimination in wages, denial of advancement in opportunities, and professional conduct, take up the banner of leadership for rights as egalitarians and end up brandishing the sword as conquistadors.

Because the meaning of egalitarianism has become evasive and ambiguous, feminine leadership that espouses it without qualification may endanger the specific cause for which it is fighting. The backlash of confusion and conquest begins on both sides, annihilating the intention for good in leadership.

Women in leadership must clearly assess their intentions and focus on definitive goals. A coalition of generic women's groups blurs that focus, diluting leadership and goading rather than guiding. The enigma of labels is prone to distract and divide (because of uncertainty or suspicion of what they stand for), rather than guide. Focused communication of the intentions and identity of leadership most effectively furthers a cause.

The Tiff About Titles

In the argument about women in leadership, both those who insist on titles and those who resist titles must look closely at their own intentions. For example, the question of whether a woman should be a pastor raises an immediate emotional response in both the liberal and traditional church. The "yeas" and "nays" are vehement. Is the controversy primarily over title, or intention?

The suggestion to separate the issues does not in any way diminish the importance of each. In fact, it emphasizes the need for the serious selection of leadership descriptions.

Vickie Kraft talks about the intention in pastoring. In reference to 1 Corinthians 12 she says:

> The gifts are given by the Holy Spirit as He chooses without discrimination based on gender. Take, for instance, the gift of pastoring. In the Greek, 'pastor' is the word 'shepherd.' I believe that there is a difference between the office and the gift, and that whereas there should be male leadership in the office of pastor, more women have the gift of pastoring than men. What is pastoring? It is feeding, caring for, and nurturing the sheep, and binding their wounds. What does that sound like? Mothering![5]

We see that the description of pastoring in and of itself certainly applies to either gender. In the same manner the title "minister" should not be problematic. Yet churches have split over the very issue of title. I know of one church that titled a woman in the full-time staff ministry "minister" then changed her title to "director." Her responsibilities and her intentions in the ministry never changed; neither did her time and labor. The dynamic that devaluated her "worth" (and diminished her salary) was a title.

The critical question with labels in leadership is the intention of the description. What does it mean? The office of pastor is usually cited as restricted to males because it is viewed as a designation of authority in addition to duties. Women in the Scriptures are not restricted from ministering. It is the assumption of feminine authority in positions of male responsibility that is controversial. Titles are not the key here; rather, we must determine what is the intention of the responsibilities in the church.

The Conduct of Leadership

Think again about your picture postcard of a woman in leadership. What would a caption reveal about her behavior? To understand how a woman in leadership assesses her intentions and identity by her conduct, we will look at three picture postcards. The first portrays boldness, the second shows subtleness, and the third reveals stereotypes.

The Bold Print

There is Mrs. Clinton on the cover of *Time*, a picture of strong confidence. There is no doubt that she is a leader. Some would caption her photo "An Aggressive Woman"; others would write "An Assertive Woman." Which would be the more positive image?

The productive leader is assertive. She communicates clearly, confidently, directly. Though the intention of an assertive message is evident and may include emotion, it is not judgmental. Aggressive leadership, on the other hand, attacks and manipulates.

The Soft Print

Mrs. Bush smiled and murmured an endearment as she leaned over to touch the arm of her grandchild. That instant was captured forever on film by a newsman. Some would caption the photo "A Soft Woman." A more descriptive title might be "A Subtle Woman."

The productive leader is subtle. She understands the importance of paralanguage. Soft, subtle communication by sound, pitch, and volume is paralanguage.

The Celebration of Womanhood

The Stereotypical Print

The cartoon character Ms. Cathy sits at her desk with a disarray of paperwork. Appearing overwrought, her eyes are enlarged, her hair on end. Some would caption that picture, "Stereotype of a Single Woman." The productive woman in leadership understands the danger of stereotyping.

The Celebration of Leadership

Our last photo, a Polaroid print, is still developing. Is that you I see emerging? The ideal woman in leadership knows her identity and understands and develops her potential. With confidence she celebrates her gifts.

She guides and provides for the good of the group. She understands organization and long-range planning. She works vigorously and makes profitable business transactions. If a task needs to be finished she will work into the night.

She is not only sensitive to her followers but responds to the needs of others around her, giving to the poor.

With assertiveness and dignity and humor and wisdom she leads her followers. She is always faithful in her intimate relationships, trusting and supporting her family and friends.

Those closest to her know the secret of her success and attractiveness—she hopes in God. She is well-known in the city and rewarded for her work. She delights in her mission. She is the woman of Proverbs 31.

Discovering Your Mission

1. What are the qualifications for feminine leadership?
2. Should women be given equal title and equal pay for equal work? Explain.

Further Research

Using resources such as Walter Liefeld and Ruth Tucker's *Daughters of the Church* and John Piper and Wayne Grudem's book, *Recovering Biblical Manhood and Womanhood*, summarize the evangelical egalitarian and traditional views regarding women in leadership. Which do you think is biblically correct? Why?

NOTES

1. Elizabeth Baker, *Wanting to Follow, Forced to Lead* (Wheaton, Ill.: Tyndale, 1991), Introduction.
2. Ibid.
3. Vickie Kraft, *Women Mentoring Women* (Chicago: Moody, 1992), 17.
4. John V. Gilmore, *The Productive Personality* (San Francisco: Albion, 1974), 33.
5. Kraft, *Women Mentoring Women*, 21.

12

Confirming Worth in the Workplace

Give her the reward she has earned, and let her works bring her praise at the city gate.

Proverbs 31:31

"Take Our Daughters to Work" day is celebrated in the comic strips as well as the workplace. Several cartoonists depict their characters debating the issue of a woman's worth in the workplace and the benefit of daughters visiting their mothers.

As early as the first grade our daughter Grace sensed something of the controversy about women leaving home for work or education. A bitter gubernatorial campaign was vividly portrayed on television news. One candidate showed video shots of his wife in the kitchen preparing supper while he worked on office papers. We were careful not to discuss our political views in front of our then small children, since my husband's position as president of a public college was much affected by state politics. So we were surprised when Grace spoke out as we were leaving the polling place.

"Didn't that one candidate believe that girls shouldn't go to college but just stay at home and have babies?" she asked.

My husband responded, "I didn't hear him say that."

"Well," she continued with emphasis, "If he did say it, that's dumb."

The Celebration of Womanhood

Grace has forgotten this conversation, but the controversy of a woman's preparation for and position in the work force continues today.

What is the primary issue of the work controversy for women with an eternal mission as well as daily responsibility to those entrusted in our care? Whereas extreme traditionalists want women to stay at home in all circumstances, the liberal attitude does not understand a woman's desire to fulfill the feminine mission. As we line up on either side of the work issue our emotions bar us from seeing the importance of confirming a woman's worth in her work. The writer of Proverbs says, "Give her the reward she has earned, and let her works bring her praise at the city gate" (31:31).

Whether a woman works in her home or in an office, as a volunteer or paid employee, we must consider the worth of her work. Women of worthy conduct should be recognized and rewarded in the workplace. We will examine the character of a woman worthy of recognition in her work, the conduct of a woman worthy of reward in her work, and the commendation of a woman worthy of public notice. We will look at the issues that a woman must face in the everyday world of employment, whether she has sought employment or is a wage earner by necessity.

Character Worthy of Recognition

Though the woman in Proverbs 31 is rightfully interpreted as the model of a good wife, that chapter also shows us the characteristics of a woman, married or single, worthy of recognition in her work both at home and in public. The qualities set forth are worthy of praise, acknowledgment, and affirmation—but not legal affirmative action. Although it is important to recognize and appreciate these qualities as they affect a woman's conduct in her work, they are not the criteria for employment or reward. (The actions of conduct

Confirming Worth in the Workplace

that we will consider in the next section are the basis for advancement and remuneration.) Proverbs 31 describes seven qualities of the woman who is worthy of personal and public affirmation: dependability, determination, sensitivity, unselfishness, purity, dignity, and delight.

Dependability

The dependable woman's work is characterized by her responsible conduct. Others can depend on her. "Her husband has full confidence in her" (v. 11). Dependability is a worthy, womanly quality, whether one is married or single. Can others depend on you? Do you plan ahead and prepare for the future? That description of the worthy woman shows that others feel secure with her management. It is certainly a quality that we should display in the work force as well as at home.

Determination

"She gets up while it is still dark. . . . She sets about her work vigorously . . . and does not eat the bread of idleness" (vv. 15, 17, 27). Qualities of determination are an asset to her character. A woman who is energetic in her work deserves affirmation.

Sensitivity

"She opens her arms to the poor and extends her hands to the needy" (v. 20). Sensitivity to the needs of others is a quality of worth in the workplace. Though she is determined, ruthlessness is not a desirable quality for success. Whether you are working to achieve something better for your family or developing your gifts for the good of a company, do not lose sight of and compassion for those who have not achieved what you have. A sensitive woman is

The Celebration of Womanhood

willing to share with others what she has learned. Her sensitivity allows her to be a model and mentor.

Unselfishness

A woman who continues to give to others as she works is worthy of affirmation. The writer of Proverbs describes her as giving to her family, to her servants, and even to strangers.

Purity

"Many women do noble things, but you surpass them all. Charm is deceptive, and beauty is fleeting; but a woman who fears the Lord is to be praised" (vv. 29–30). That is an indication of the motive of a woman's work. The deception of charm implies manipulation. Fear of the Lord implies the pure motive of honoring God in one's work.

Dignity

"She is clothed with strength and dignity" (v. 25). Dignity means a professional attitude, a serious acceptance of the task at hand. Our dress, our speech, and our attention to a task reveal our level of respect.

Does it matter how you dress for the job? Perhaps clothes do not change the quality of your work, but they do say something about the dignity you assign to it. If your employment requires casual attire, is it clean? Do you wear it proudly?

Delight

"She can laugh at the days to come" (v. 25). That is the second half of the verse about dignity. This woman not only refuses to worry because she is prepared, but she doesn't take her strength and dignity too seriously. She knows a balance and enjoys her work.

Confirming Worth in the Workplace

A woman should be appreciated and affirmed for each of those qualities. They are to be respected by both her family and her employers. Though the lack of those qualities may affect the product of her work, it is her performance, not her effort, on which affirmative action should be based.

Conduct Worthy of Reward

Affirmative action is the assertion that if a group of people are underrepresented in the work force, society has the obligation to assure their representation. In other words, the employer must actively seek qualified women candidates for a position if women are underrepresented in that company. In truth, however, affirmative action must be joined with qualifications. It is for these qualifications that a woman should be equally rewarded, as the writer of Proverbs states. "Give her the reward she has earned" (31:31).

Civil rights is defined as the right one has to take legal action if there has been discrimination because of race, religion, sex, or age. Some extreme groups interpret affirmative action as an obligation to hire, regardless of qualifications, judging a woman worthy wholly on the basis of her sex. Such groups demand the reward of employment as a civil right regardless of performance. The current interpretation of the law agrees with the Scripture that a woman earns her reward by the quality of her work.

Six qualities directly affect a woman's performance in her work and may be used as a criteria for reward. The woman in Proverbs 31 demonstrates these attributes: qualification by skill, by intelligence, by preparation, by experience, by wisdom, and by communication.

Qualification by Skill

Proverbs 31:13–24 refer to a woman's skill not only as a buyer but as a manufacturer and merchandiser of clothing.

She shows a demonstrated qualification of skill. She has references.

Proverbs 22:29 concurs with the value of skill: "Do you see a man [woman] skilled in his [her] work? He [she] will serve before kings; he [she] will not serve before obscure men."

Development of skill and the development of gifts are often synonymous. Our friends the Murk Family Singers are an example of faithfulness to the development of gifts. Each of their five children was given daily instruction and disciplined in the practice of voice and musical instruments. As a result of the growth of those skills they earned the reward of full-time employment as musicians. They are able to do that not because they were born with natural ability but because they continue to qualify by the progression of their skill.

Qualified by Intelligence

"She considers a field and buys it; out of her earnings she plants a vineyard" (Proverbs 31:16). That statement indicates an application of intelligence in the transaction of business. She considers, weighs options, and invests in her property. She is a woman capable of assessment, making decisions, and implementing those decisions. That verse could well describe a businesswoman in today's world.

It doesn't say anything about clearing her decision with a man. She displays intelligence and is free to negotiate on her own. She faces a bigger decision than merely going to the grocery store. She understands and handles a legal transaction on her own. A demonstration of intelligence is a qualification for reward in the workplace. Women were obviously active in business life in Israel three thousand years ago. It should not surprise us to see Christian women effectively serving businesses today based on their strong qualifications.

Qualified by Preparation

"Her arms are strong for her tasks. . . . When it snows, she has no fear for her household; for all of them are clothed in scarlet" (vv. 17, 21). That implies preparation. She keeps herself in good physical condition by preparing good food, even acquiring it from afar (v. 14). She uses her mind to plan ahead, preparing for needs that will probably arise, such as inclement weather.

Martha was widowed at midlife and was at a loss as to how she would spend the rest of her life. She had enjoyed a good marriage but was not ready to seek another life partner. Her sister Margaret suggested that she prepare for a career.

"At my age?" she replied, "By the time I am prepared with bachelor and master's degrees, I'll be ready to retire."

But at the time Margaret served as a trustee at Henry Ford Community College, which offered a two-year medical records program. Martha enrolled through the Focus on Women counseling and financial aid program. She discovered she was eligible for a federal grant.

In two years she graduated with honors. Martha became director of medical records at one of Detroit's hospitals and was financially compensated far beyond her expectations. A woman who is adequately prepared for employment will see the reward of qualification.

Another aspect of qualification could be described as mental focus. That involves attention to organization. It also includes the discipline of being mentally present. Do you adequately organize your personal affairs so that you can concentrate at work? The qualified woman disciplines her mind to focus on the present. That can apply to work in the home as well. It does not mean you cannot dream; however, it does define the attention span given to work.

Qualified by Experience

"She sees that her trading is profitable, and her lamp does not go out at night" (v. 18). Her experience is profitable. Therefore she continues to build upon that experience. A woman's experience in business is valuable both to her and to her employer. It is a desirable qualification for building future business.

Qualified by Wisdom

"She speaks with wisdom, and faithful instruction is on her tongue" (v. 26). This is an inferred qualification. Wisdom comes with knowledge, and instruction that is faithful keeps growing in knowledge.

My mother was a marvelous example of a woman who turned her ear to wisdom, so that faithful instruction was on her tongue. Her devotion to Scripture throughout her life was the key to her wisdom. Her Bible was never far from her, and Scripture was principally used to encourage, support, and inspire. Encouraging verses appeared on mirrors, in books, and in letters. That wisdom grew and endured to her last moments when she looked ahead and said, "I see heaven. It's celestial, beautiful—with high technology."

Qualified by Communication

Her ability to buy and sell, to make a profitable trade, to speak, and to instruct involves communication. To accomplish those tasks she must be able to speak assertively. Assertiveness boldly objects to harassment and clearly articulates needs and proposals. It is a direct, nonhostile expression of true thoughts and feelings.

Commendation Worthy of Public Notice

The proverbial epilogue about a woman of noble character begins and ends with commendation. A woman of "noble character who can find? She is worth far more than rubies. . . . Give her the reward she has earned, and let her works bring her praise at the city gate." (vv. 1, 31).

Affirmation, praise, and appreciation are appropriately given to women of noble character. You should earn personal respect in the workplace for dependability, determination, sensitivity, unselfishness, purity, dignity, and delight in your work.

Equal pay, equal promotions, and equal employment should be given to women of worthy conduct. This choice of conduct should qualify you as you demonstrate skill, intelligence, preparation, experience, and education, and as you assertively communicate your ideas.

I might note that just as the man is respected at the city gate, so is the woman to be praised at the city gate. Public note of a woman's worth is biblical.

Discovering Your Mission

1. What qualities of a woman does the writer of Proverbs 31 describe that should bring her personal and public affirmation? Do you agree with him? Are there others?

2. What is the difference between affirmation and affirmative action?

3. What qualifications are important for advancement in the workplace?

4. What qualities and qualifications help you to celebrate the feminine mission? Why?

Further Research

Investigate a court case that illustrates gender discrimination and the need for affirmative action in the workplace. Explain whether you agree or disagree with the judgment and why. What were the defendant's qualifications, and how did they compare with the ideal in Proverbs 31?

13

Confirming Opportunities as Friends

*Perfume and incense bring joy to the heart,
and the pleasantness of one's friend springs from
[her] earnest counsel.*

Proverbs 27:9

The scent of perfume, the pleasant and gratifying fragrance that often adorns a woman, was an important part of worship in the time of Moses. Fine spices, liquid myrrh, cinnamon, cassia, and olive oil were blended by a perfumer. Incense was also made with the fragrance of the spices—gum resin, onycha, and galbanum—and blended with pure frankincense.

A perfumer works diligently to make a pleasing fragrance. The work involves not only the perfect blending of just the right formula but knowing how to extract the pure, raw ingredients from flower petals, mosses, and leaves. He knows which plants need to be crushed to yield higher concentrates of pure oil; which should be treated in a more gentle fashion, stirred with a solvent and distilled; and which should be percolated, like coffee beans, until the plant or petal exhausts all of its perfume.

Moses was instructed by the Lord to make a special blend of perfume and another of incense, a fragrance so pure and pleasant that it was not ever to be used or imitated by the people. It was a sacred formula, only to be used in consecrating the priests, the Tent of Meeting, the ark of tes-

The Celebration of Womanhood

timony, the table and its articles, the lampstand and its accessories, the altar of incense, the altar of burnt offering and its utensils, and the basin with its stand.

The fragrance was a sacred symbol of God's holiness, of His presence, of what belonged to Him. The people were not allowed to splash the perfume on themselves—not even a drop. In fact, if anyone used or copied the formula he or she was put to death. An environmental waste? No, it was a sweet smelling sacrifice to God. The people were reminded of His holiness—by the sweet scent of that symbol—as they were drawn to the place of holiness.

We all know the powerful attractiveness of a sweet fragrance. Your favorite perfume is probably different from mine. You experiment with just the right amount, the blend that is right for you. Some scents are repugnant because they were not thoroughly processed. Usually the most expensive ones, the most difficult to process, are the most dear to us.

Our lives are like the blend of a complicated formula of raw materials. Our personal fragrance is the result of how we have processed the difficult passages in our lives. Some of us who have been crushed emit a bitter scent forever. Others accept the circumstances of the process and eventually spread an overwhelmingly attractive fragrance. Like a flower, our reaction to the blend of circumstances in our lives determines our personal fragrance.

The fragrance of some women's lives is so attractive to us that we start to follow their formula, thinking maybe it will work for us. Perhaps those women have experienced something that we are experiencing or wish to experience. They are victorious survivors of a passage in life or a process of achievement or defeat. They may have passed through grief or loss or illness or struggle and yet still achieved personal goals or exhibited deep contentment, for-

Confirming Opportunities as Friends

titude, and perseverance. They are women who have accomplished something that others want to accomplish—through faith, skill, and personal relationships. They become our models.

Women are empowered to share the meaning of their lives and their mission through their fragrance and faithful friendships. In this chapter, we will examine the double power of our fragrance and faithful friendships and discover how the fragrance of our lives is processed and possessed. We will show how faithful friendships empower us to encourage, counsel, disciple, and mentor.

The Power of Our Fragrance

A model is:

- a real person whom you know or know about
- a person whose behavior you admire or imitate
- a person whose conduct is consistent and not dependent on who is watching her

It is possible that someone is attracted to the fragrance of your life, even though you do not know that person. Amy Carmichael, the single woman who founded the Donheaver Fellowship in India, continues to serve as a model woman even though she died in 1951. Her integrity and courage, perseverance, and creativity first inspired me as a teenager. For more than three decades, I have read and reread her poems. Though I never knew her personally, I admire the lingering fragrance of her life, the example of her conduct, the practical ways in which she demonstrated her hope in God.

We all have a fragrance. Some fragrances are sweeter, some stronger, some a little sour. Whether we like it or not, the world smells our fragrance. Can we do anything about how we smell? Do we have any control of the process?

The Process

One of a woman's greatest frustrations is the perceived lack of control in her life. Control is sometimes labeled as evil by those who interpret Eve's sin as the desire to control. "Give up control," we are told. "Just trust God and men as the controllers."

But wait. As both women and men go through the process of life, passing through both desirable and undesirable circumstances, they are equally responsible for their actions and reactions. Men are given no greater power in controlling the unplanned, unexpected, uncalled for circumstances in life than women. Though some men have interpreted their designated responsibility "to rule" as control, neither men nor women are to control the minds and hearts of another human being. It is the confusion on this issue that sustains cults such as the Davidians who died in Waco, Texas.

Women who think they have no control become bitter or bland. We back away from them and avoid them because we can't get past the barrier of their acrid odor.

Think of the fragrance of a family. Each member, though sharing many similar circumstances, develops his or her individual scent. Though the parents "rule"—protecting, guiding, providing, even maneuvering some circumstances—the children are held responsible for their behavior.

When a woman gives her life to a man or to God it does not mean that she loses all control of her life. Such a life is malodorous. The process of a woman giving her life to a man or to God is almost the opposite. She controls the choice to yield herself to a man or God, voluntarily submitting to another's protection, guidance, and provision. She continually controls her choice of submission. Though she makes an initial commitment to do so, she is responsible for daily controlling her conduct. It is that decision of self-discipline that Paul meant when he said, "Let us be self-controlled" (1 Thessalonians 5:8). Similarly, Jesus spoke of controlling ourselves when He said, "If anyone would come after me, he must deny himself and take up his cross and follow me" (Matthew 16:24).

Control is the discipline of looking beyond self, looking beyond the unpleasantness of a circumstance. It sometimes means yielding. It sometimes means resisting. It means trusting someone other than yourself.

Every woman must decide for herself how she will respond to the circumstances of life. Should she yield, resist, or trust? When she puts her hope in God, the One who knows the perfect formula for the fragrance of her life, she spreads the sweet-smelling aroma of Christ.

> But thanks be to God, who always leads us in triumphal procession in Christ and through us spreads everywhere the fragrance of the knowledge of him. For we are to God the aroma of Christ among those who are being saved and those who are perishing. To the one we are the smell of death; to the other, the fragrance of life. (2 Corinthians 2:14–16)

The Possession

This fragrance, the aroma of Christ, is to be treasured. As it was in the time of Moses, it is still a symbol of God's holiness. It is to be shared. In a symbolic gesture of devotion one woman came to Jesus and poured an expensive alabaster jar of perfume upon His head. The people who saw her were indignant.

"Why this waste of perfume?" they asked. "It could have been sold for more than a year's wages and the money given to the poor" (Mark 14:4).

Jesus saw her gesture as an act of worship, a sacrificial gift of her fragrance, a sign of her recognition of His holiness and her deliberate decision to put her hope in Him. He said:

> Leave her alone. . . . Why are you bothering her? She has done a beautiful thing to me. The poor you will always have with you, and you can help them any time you want. But you will not always have me. She did what she could. She poured perfume on my body beforehand to prepare for my burial. I tell you the truth, wherever the gospel is preached throughout the world, what she has done will also be told, in memory of her. (Mark 14:6–9)

That woman was a model of submission to Christ. Every woman models a fragrance—pure or diluted, sweet or sour or bland. Public figures sometimes have the opportunity to share the formula—the story—of their fragrance. However, it is through faithful friendships that we are all empowered to personally share the fragrance of our lives.

The Power of Our Friendships

Friends are people you know, like, and trust. The Scripture narrows the concept of friend to one who loves you at all times (Proverbs 17:17).

Abraham was given the remarkable compliment of being called God's friend. He believed God when He promised that Abraham would father a child. Because he believed he was called God's friend.

When someone believes us, trusts us, and loves us, she wants to know what we are made of. In the confidence of

Confirming Opportunities as Friends

friendship we have the opportunity to reveal the contents of our hearts, the fragrance of our lives. With Paul we might ask, "And who is equal to such a task?" (2 Corinthians 2:16).

The wise woman speaks with sincerity, honoring her friendships, listening to the heart of her friend. She knows when to encourage, when to counsel, when to disciple, when to mentor.

With each new level of intimacy in our friendships, we are able to share more of ourselves. One way to evaluate the appropriate level of sharing in a friendship would be to rate the relationship in terms of contact, confidence, commitment, and compatibility.

Contact relates to the length of time you have known the person and how frequently you see her.

Confidence relates to how well you know the person. Usually meaningful disclosure is a gradual process. Rate the relationship from one to ten in terms of the depth of confidences that you have shared.

Commitment is the level of trust or belief that you have in your friend and that your friend has in you. Perhaps you completely trust another in an isolated area, such as babysitting your children, but you are not sure you would trust her with your credit card. We tend to commit ourselves to segments of other people. A discreet woman is careful about her commitments. However, the wider our range of commitment is, the broader is our opportunity for sharing the fragrance of our lives with another.

Compatibility is the last factor in assessing our friendships. Do you like each other? The greater the pleasure you find in one another's company, the greater will be your compatibility.

Those four categories are merely a tool for helping us understand the appropriate level of giving in our relationships. Since growing relationships are dynamic, changing every day, those factors will change each day. For instance, though mentorship programs are devised as a way of pairing a mentor and protégé, the actual process of mentoring could be termed the most intimate level of sharing. A real mentor goes through all the preliminary steps—encouraging, counseling, and discipling. Mentorship involves all of those and more. To understand the differences in those activities and how they relate to friendship we will examine them one by one.

The Process of Encouragement

This process in friendship can begin right away. In fact, it may be the reason that a friendship begins. To give encouragement is to support or to inspire hope. Everyone can learn to be an encourager by doing one or more of the following.

Listening. In Psalm 10:17 we read the example of the Lord's encouragement by listening. "You hear, O Lord, the desire of the afflicted; you encourage them, and you listen to their cry."

Our children always refer to our friends Sue and Jerry as aunt and uncle. Probably the biggest reason that they feel as though they are related to Sue and Jerry is that the couple listens to them. As a result, our children, even as teenagers, love to talk to these dear friends. Sue and Jerry hear, they respond (our kids especially like to hear "Uncle" Jerry laugh), and they care about what is being said.

Listening is not only the first step in establishing a friendship; it is the sustenance of a lasting relationship.

Spending time. Two leaders in the New Testament church, Judas (Barabbas) and Silas, took time out of their busy travel schedules to spend time with the church in Antioch. Acts 15:32–33 reports their encouraging words. I am sure their encouragement went beyond words. Their presence also strengthened the church.

Words are not always necessary. Spending time with someone can bring encouragement. Time is a precious commodity, which is why giving up some of your time for a friend is a gift.

Using our gifts. By developing our gifts and using them, we can encourage others. Romans 12:1–8 tells us to use sober judgment in this area and not to think of ourselves more highly than we ought to. The leader can encourage by leading diligently. The one who shows mercy can encourage by doing it cheerfully. The ones who like to contribute can encourage by giving generously. It is the attitude with which we use our gifts that encourages others.

Recounting experiences. Twice Paul sent his friend Tychicus to encourage the church with a firsthand account of his experiences, once to Ephesus and once to Colossae.

You can encourage someone by keeping in touch or communicating firsthand. When friends are secretive and silent, we often become discouraged. That is especially true in close relationships. Your willingness to share your life can be a gift of encouragement to another.

Sharing faith. Paul was on a preaching tour, exhausted and stressed. He had been to Thessalonica and was persecuted for preaching and forced to leave. The hostile atmosphere made him anxious for those he left behind. Maybe his efforts were useless. When he couldn't stand it any longer he sent Timothy to Thessalonica to check on his friends. Timothy returned with good news. He told Paul that his friends had good memories of him and that they were anxious to see him. Most encouraging, though, was the report that they were standing firm in their faith in the Lord. "We were encouraged . . . because of your faith," Paul wrote the Thessalonians. We can encourage others by standing firm in the faith.

Sharing knowledge. The knowledge of sound doctrine is also a means of encouragement. This is affirmed in 1 Thessalonians 4:18 and Titus 1:9. Knowledge dispels confusion and clarifies direction. The sharing of spiritual knowledge should be a natural activity, certainly an encouraging activity.

Building up. The most obvious way of encouraging others is by affirming them. It is, however, the most difficult action for some. Why? We are afraid we will be misunderstood. We might be labeled as gushy or manipulative. Many times we avoid affirming another because we think that person already knows how we feel. But if you say nothing, she may feel taken for granted.

Again, to the Thessalonians, Paul spoke of encouragement. He urged them to encourage each other and build each other up. The most effective affirmations are brief, specific, and delivered as a gift—not as statements that require response.

Supporting the timid. "Encourage the timid," the Scripture declares (1 Thessalonians 5:14). My friend Marian, a master teacher, exemplifies that application. She teaches speech, a class universally feared by students. Though it is considered a freshman level course, many students put off taking it until their senior year. Knowing that, yet understanding the value of learning the skill of public speaking, Marian has devised a curriculum that encourages the timid. Each student is supported by a small group. They plan together, practice together, and perform together. By the time the student is required to speak before a large group, he or she has been bolstered by a personal cheering squad.[1]

Look for creative ways to encourage the timid.

Sharing food. The storm was so vicious that all 276 passengers on board the ship in the Adriatic Sea forgot about eating. They were in constant suspense, fearing they would be drowned or dashed against rocks. Paul was a passenger on that ship, and after fourteen days he urged everyone to eat. "You need it to survive," he said. They were encouraged, and they ate (Acts 27:34).

The simple action of eating together is encouraging. It may be the food, the camaraderie, the leveling effect of the table—or the acknowledgment that we are all the same in our need of sustenance.

Single people will tell you that eating alone in a restaurant is difficult. It is discouraging. The custom of breaking bread together is universally appealing. Instead of dropping off a casserole, arrange to eat with your friend. Is it too much work? Too expensive? We often share our dinner at home. I call a friend and say, "Would you like to combine dinners on Sunday?" Some of the most encouraging times that we have spent with friends have been over a simple meal. There is a bond in eating together, an intimacy that affirms our relationships.

Visiting. Friends from Rome traveled as far as the Forum of Appius and the Three Taverns to visit Paul. "At the sight of these men Paul thanked God and was encouraged" (Acts 28:14–15).

When our son Jon was eleven years old he was hit by a car that flipped off a curve and flattened him on the sidewalk before careening into a bridge. Though no bones were broken, the flesh was torn from his legs, and he was left black and blue and bedridden for several weeks. Everyone who made a special visit to see Jon brought him encouragement.

It is the effort of dropping by for ten or fifteen minutes that means so much. It is a way of saying, "You are important to me. I wanted to see you." If you feel it is more appropriate, call ahead and ask if you can say hello.

Accepting. When we are able to accept and rise above difficult circumstances in our lives, we are a model of encouragement to others. Paul realized that others were encouraged to speak the words of God when they saw him praise God, even in imprisonment. In this kind of encouragement it is not so much what we say that encourages but the way we live. People will see peace and be encouraged.

Working. Paul worked hard—he labored—so that the people in Laodicea would be encouraged in their hearts (Colossians 2:1–2). Our labors can encourage others.

The Process of Counseling

Numerous texts and popular books about counseling are available for study. Though it is not necessary to repeat counseling techniques here, we will briefly summarize the definition of counseling in friendships. Counseling in the setting of friendship involves listening, learning needs, looking together at a problem, and leading thoughts.

Listening. Listening means focusing outside of ourselves, on the words of our friend, the nonverbal clues of intonation, volume, pace, and gestures, hearing the heart of our friend.

Learning needs. Learning needs, as discussed in chapter 6, often involves asking questions and paraphrasing.

Looking together. By looking together at a problem we begin to help our friend develop options or strategic solutions. At that point the counseling friend might suggest that more information should be gathered or that waiting for a period of time might reveal a new solution for the problem.

Leading thoughts. The wise listening friend will not merely advise but will guide the conversation in such a way as to develop new thoughts.

The Process of Discipling

A disciple not only looks for counsel from a friend but follows her in a discipline of study. A disciple makes a commitment of consistent time to learn a specific subject from her model. Though Scripture mentions repeatedly the need to be a disciple, only once does it tell us to make disciples—in Matthew 28:19. The action of making disciples involves evangelism and teaching. That definition might apply to both secular and spiritual discipleship. As friends are drawn to the fragrance of our lives, we teach them how to follow in the same way.

The popular phrase "I am discipling someone" can be misleading. Particularly in the Christian world, the emphasis on self as the discipler draws away from the intention of Jesus to make disciples *of Him*. That distinction must be clear. We should not be disciples of an individual who is teaching and leading us spiritually, but as equal individuals *we* are to be disciples of the One about whom *we* are teaching.

In the secular vein there is less of a distinction. One may be not only a disciple of the discipline itself but of the one teaching. Here the term is used in the more generic sense to mean "student of." Whether in the sacred or secular world, the relationship between the disciple and her friend is more intense than that of a encourager or counselor.

The Process of Mentoring

"Mentor" was actually the name of a male character in Greek mythology. In *Telemaque,* the writer-philosopher Fenelon cast Mentor as the trusted adviser and friend of Telemachus, the son of Odysseus. Mentor was Telemachus's wise counselor in the absence of his father. A person characterized as a mentor is, in general, a trusted counselor and friend—like Mentor. The specific application of the term mentor is more subtle and significant. The ideal mentor is

1. a model—as described previously—who personally interacts over a period of time with a person who seeks the mentor's counsel
2. a person of experience who gives wise advice to one with less experience (usually one who is younger)
3. a person who is sought after by others for counsel

Intimate friendships among women are sometimes confused with the mentor relationship. The mentor relationship is the most intense level of friendship. The mentor, usually older and more experienced in the area of mentorship, does more than casually discuss her experiences. As she teaches, she watches, prompts, and often provides for and protects the one who is following her. The mentor relationship is based upon unequal experience but complete confidence and open communication.

The bond of the mentor relationship is personal but may be limited to the sharing of life experiences in a specific area of common interest. To assume or allow an emotional —or romantic—attachment beyond that of simple friendship usually destroys the mentor relationship, whether the mentor is male or female.

Though the opportunity to begin a mentoring relationship may come through introductions, information, and the activities of a program, mentoring is not based on a role one plays but on a relationship. It is one's attitude and availability to progress through the levels of friendship that open or close the doors to mentorship.

Often the counsel that a mentor provides develops so naturally from a relationship of confidence and trust that a woman doesn't even realize that she is considered a mentor. The true mentor doesn't offer her advice as a matter of duty or a determination to do a good deed but shows the way out of devotion to the way and the woman.

Perhaps you are willing to share the fragrance of your life by encouraging, counseling, discipling, or mentoring, but that initial step of making a connection with a new friend is awkward. Below are four avenues for developing new friendships: giving of yourself to the church, giving of yourself to women with special needs, giving of yourself in family relationships, and giving of yourself in the community.

Giving to the church. Vickie Kraft's book *Women Mentoring Women* is an in-depth practical guide for the development of a variety of women's programs sponsored by the church.[2] If you are looking for ideas to begin a vital women's ministry, you will want this book.

Giving to women with special needs. Mary Gates Somerville, in *Mentor Moms,* has written a specialized program for ministering to teen mothers.[3] Because of her background as a former staff member of Young Life and pastor's wife in California, she was approached by Young Life to develop a program for unwed teen mothers. In *Mentor Moms* she writes about her experiences in beginning the program, including practical details and guidelines for new programs.

Giving yourself in family relationships. Our family relationships are often the most difficult areas in which to emit our fragrance. The sweetest aroma will be spread by genuine loving actions.

Giving of yourself in the community. The seed ideas for women's outreach into the community are also planted in *Women Mentoring Women.* They include: Uplifters—"a support ministry through which women who have had breast cancer support breast cancer patients and their families";

outreach to dysfunctional families; mom-to-mom programs; hospitality volunteers for newcomers; hospital visitation; and tutoring in the inner city.[4]

Through the fragrance of our lives we celebrate the feminine mission, confirming the reality of our eternal purpose through faithful friendships.

Discovering Your Mission

1. What actions of others are most encouraging to you? Why?
2. Is there a special action of encouragement that comes easily to you? How do you use it?
3. What is the difference between a mentor and a model? How can you become one of those?

Further Research

Write a brief biographical sketch of a woman who is a model or mentor to women. What is the fragrance of her life that attracted you or others?

Notes

1. Marian Tyndale Carter, *Content & Delivery, The Dichotomy of Public Speaking* (Beaumont, Calif.: Maple Leaf, 1993).
2. Vickie Kraft, *Women Mentoring Women* (Chicago: Moody, 1992).
3. Mary Gates Somerville, *Mentor Moms* (1819 E. Seeger Court, Visalia, Calif., 93277, 1992).
4. Kraft, *Women Mentoring Women*, 149.

14

Confirming Authenticity in Diverse Communities

> *Each one should use whatever gift [she] has
> received to serve others,
> faithfully administering God's grace in its various
> forms.*
>
> 1 Peter 4:10

Mee's marriage at thirteen to twenty-year-old Xiong was encouraged by relatives in the California town of Merced they call home. Both Mee and Xiong, who live with Xiong's parents, are proud that they are continuing in school—she in the seventh grade, he in community college. Their early marriage is in keeping with the Hmong custom that urges men to find very young wives and father many children.[1]

Approximately 100,000 Hmong have immigrated to the United States since the late 1970s. Some of the Hmong customs are radically different from those in the united States. Polygamy is practiced among some Hmong. The birth of a male child is highly cherished. Some Hmong children, like Choula, a seventeen-year-old high school girl, are resisting cultural customs such as early marriage. She wants to go to college and make her own decision about getting married. But she isn't ready to be completely assimilated. She cites the good things about the Hmong ways—taking care of the older generation, the language, customs, and music.

Though the Hmong are among us, they are different. They are more "other" than "us." Agencies such as the

The Celebration of Womanhood

U.S. Center for World Mission in Pasadena, California, are reaching out to the Hmong people with the biblical message. The Center's proposal goes beyond the communication of words, religious conversion, or cultural change; it is attempting to form a community of otherness.[2]

Diversity is otherness; it includes something or someone not like us, different than we are. The differences may be in background, ethnic origin, physical capabilities, education, genetics, age, customs, or even values.

Community is forming a oneness, drawing together, strengthening, supporting, and attaining a growth that is greater than the sum of individual growth. The true meaning of community is deeper than an organizational structure; it touches the soul of each member.

A community of otherness is, therefore, a group of diverse people who draw together in spirit and action for a common goal or for the good of all. A woman's relationship to her communities of otherness confirms the reality of her commitment to the feminine mission. In this chapter we will explore the impact of that relationship by examining five aspects of its meaning: the conflict—tension with the community of otherness; the concept—communicating in the communities of otherness; the concurrences—identification with the communities of otherness; the conduct—commitment to the communities of otherness; and the celebration—enjoyment with the communities of otherness.

The Conflict: Tension with the Community of Otherness

Professor Maurice Friedman proposes the concepts of the community of affinity and the community of otherness in *The Confirmation of Otherness*. At first, his interpretations appear harsh. He believes: "Community of affinity, or like-mindedness, is always ultimately false community. Community of otherness, in contrast, is a way of being faithful and diverse at the same time."[3] It is the implication of "false" that blurs his definition, however. The community of affinity, which he sees as people grouped as a result of agreement on a common issue, could be termed "false" in the sense that their affinity is based on only one or a few issues. An example might be a political party, a nationality, even a church. Their affinity may or may not go beyond the issue of politics or birthplace. To presume then that they fit our definition of community is false.

In reality, we could say that all communities—in the truest sense—are diverse, are communities of otherness. No two people bring exactly the same likemindedness in all areas to the group. For purposes of our discussion, however, diversity is used in the sense of issues of gender and educational, physical, racial, and cultural differences. All attempts to make a community, then, whether of a lesser or a greater degree, encounter conflict.

The Tension of "Invisibility"

Women who desire to be a part of a community, whether it be acceptance in a club or a fraternal business group, complain not only of harassment, but more often of their apparent invisibility. They are ignored, overlooked, as if they did not exist. Those who desire to form a true community of otherness must accept the reality of the tension of invisibility and be willing to work past it.

The Tension of Ignorance

Tension between individuals who are of different educational backgrounds divides followers of many great causes. Sometimes the more experienced or knowledgeable shun the novice, and sometimes it is the other way around. The prejudice of ignorance is displayed among the educated and uneducated, the experienced and inexperienced. Both can sink into conflict out of ignorance of the other's way. The problem evolves from the belief that diversity is wrong. In an attempt to dissolve all differences a line of judgment is drawn that precludes the formation of community.

The Tension of Capability

The conflict of physical or mental differences need not deter us from making a community. It may be from arrogance but is probably from ignorance and perhaps laziness that some segregate people according to their physical and mental capabilities.

I remember a man named Steve whose sweet spirit, joyous humor, and creative mind energized us each time we met at a summer conference in Michigan. Though a physical disability slowed his speech, his difference became a stimulating part of our community rather than a diversion. His ability to look beyond what made him different allowed us to do the same.

The Tension of Color

Color coding—or stereotyping individuals according to the pigment of their skin—is perhaps at once the most intense and the most superficial conflict in community. It denies personal identity, classifying a person's behavior, value, and worth according to a color code.

We have experienced this tension in the response of others who were curious or confused about the diversity in our family. It took me a long time to figure out why our son didn't like to go to church when we were on vacation. Because his ethnic origins differ from those of our girls, others were constantly pressing him to defend his place in our family. In turn, he felt displaced in the church. Comments such as, "You should be so grateful," made him feel that his difference made a barrier to his acceptance in the community of our family, as well as the greater community of that particular church.

Another tension within the community of otherness that may or may not be related to color is culture.

The Tension of Culture

Cultural diversity is the most common cause of conflict in community making. It is the most significant factor that divides one ethnic group from another, nation from nation, one denomination from another, one generation from the preceding generation. It causes significant tension among theologians today, and it was a reason for the criticism of Peter in Acts 10 and 11.

Cornelius, a centurion in the Italian regiment, asked Peter to do something that was against Jewish law. He invited Peter to his home, as his guest, because he wanted to know more about Jesus Christ. Gentile and Jewish cultures—their customs, laws, heritage, everything about them—were completely different from one another. Though Peter followed God's leading in talking with Cornelius, he was caught in a cultural clash between his old friends, the apostles, and his new friends, the Gentile believers.

In that experience Peter learned that diversity need not divide. He said, "I now realize how true it is that God does not show favoritism but accepts men from every nation who fear him and do what is right. You know the message God sent to the people of Israel, telling the good news of peace through Jesus Christ, who is Lord of all" (Acts 10:34–36). Peter saw that community making does not require sameness of culture.

My husband and I have both experienced enrichment from years of intimate interaction with personal friends who are part of the Hispanic culture. Rather than seeing diversity as divisive, we believe that it has stimulated and enlarged our vision and caused us to form a stronger intentional bond in pursuit of common goals.

The Concept:
Communicating in the Communities of Otherness

M. Scott Peck speaks to community in his book *The Different Drum: Community Making and Peace.* He explains that, "In community, instead of being ignored, denied, hidden, or changed, human differences are celebrated as gifts."[4]

The picture of the process of community making and progressive celebration may be compared to that of a marriage. In the beginning of a relationship, two different people begin to dream of possibilities; they come to a proposal; it is confirmed with engagement, sealed by marriage, and celebrated by the signpost of anniversaries.

The Possibilities

Every woman who seeks to follow the feminine mission must reach out beyond herself—beyond the comfort of affinity—and, accepting the tension of diversity, confirm the reality of her belief and behavior in a community of otherness. As in a marriage, the possibilities for involvement are multiple, but in the finite realm of time she must intentionally commit herself to a specific group or groups of people.

Her first step, then, is to become aware of others, to listen, look, and see who they are as individuals and seek to understand their needs, behavior, and culture. When you begin to appreciate your differences, you can begin to dream of possibilities.

The Proposal

Can you be part of a community? When you have shed your assumptions, your anger, and your judgments, and have honestly opened yourself to the community, overcoming the fear of vulnerability and verifying the acceptance of your identities, you are ready for the proposal.

This is a difficult step because it tests the reality of your relationship. It is perhaps the most delicate time in the process of making community because we are prone to measure differences instead of shared beliefs and dreams.

We were part of a good experience in community making during the last few years we lived in Michigan. Our church of more than two thousand members was divided into smaller groups by Sunday school class and within those groups into randomly assigned "care groups" of approximately ten family units each. We were fairly diverse—single and married, from a range of educational backgrounds, widely different in our life experiences. Our leaders were Harry and Sally, who were willing but not anxious to be responsible. From the beginning we decided to be an informal group, meeting for potluck dinners and supporting each other's needs.

If Harry and Sally had been experienced group leaders, we might have missed—all of us—the incredible, almost mystical occurrence of becoming a community of otherness. A trained group leader might have pushed a regimented format, exercises in group dynamics, a prescribed Bible study, and a broader outreach of prayer. With all of our differences we might have reshuffled the group. Or Harry and Sally and the rest of us might have given up.

At one point I was tempted to. I felt silly revealing myself. How would anyone understand? I wondered. But one night it happened. We went beyond probing possibilities and dared to risk a proposal. Each one told the others how he or she was feeling. It was an action of mutual, total submission of ourselves.

The Celebration of Womanhood

M. Scott Peck refers to that period in community making as "emptiness." I prefer to think of it as the way one feels after making a proposal of marriage. You finally release your deepest feelings and wait for a response. "Expectation" would seem more appropriate than "emptiness."

The Engagement

Due to the loving hearts and persistence of Harry and Sally, we all stayed together that night. And one by one the hopes and dreams of each one was confirmed by the group. We became a community. We were engaged forever in allegiance to one another. From then on our task was joyous. What would we commit to do together?

As a group we supported a high school student from Central America, each family treating him as part of the family. For the first part of his year in Michigan he lived with us. Later he lived with Harry and Sally and traveled with them to the East Coast. Through the financial support of our small group he attended the private school sponsored by our church.

The Marriage

It was the custom to rotate "care groups" at the end of a year. We all appealed to stay together. We were just beginning to discover the joy of this marriage—of community. But the next year, realizing that we had become so like-minded that we needed to reach out again to a new community, we accepted our assignments in new "care groups." But our "old" group never dissolved its relationship.

The Anniversaries

We still meet for reunions. We continue to be diverse. Our differences only intensify the dynamic joy of our oneness. It is cause for celebration.

While accepting the tension of diversity and sharing the dream of community, our group discovered the elements of commonality.

The Concurrences: Identification with the Communities of Otherness

At this point you are ready to identify the areas of common ground. There are three imperatives for making community. The first is to measure shared beliefs and values. Does that mean that a Christian and a Jew, holding different beliefs, cannot consider connecting in a community? It depends upon the agreed purpose of the community. You must measure your beliefs and values and their relationship to the proposed purpose. Perhaps the common values of each faith will strengthen the execution of your proposal. Then you have the possibility of community. If, on the other hand, your values and beliefs on differing points are critical to the specific proposal of growth for the community, you must seek a new common goal.

The second imperative is to agree on meeting needs. Two cultures are likely to see the needs of a common group of people as different. Patience is important here. Watch, learn, and listen. Time may show the needs to be different than you thought.

The third imperative is to make a future. The joy of community is invigorating, but it is not sustained without action. Just as in a proposed marriage, a community must have a vision of the future.

You are now engaged in these common pursuits, measuring shared beliefs, meeting needs, and making a future. How do you become a community? Like one wanting to be married, the desire for community will not be fulfilled without commitment.

The Conduct:
Commitment to the Communities of Otherness

Commitment involves giving, mainly giving of ourselves. Five specific gifts of self are part of community making.

The first is the gift of intentions. Especially in a diverse community, your words and actions must be intentional. There is no room for thoughtless, accidental, or joking remarks or activities. It is important to plan, prepare, and discuss openly but thoughtfully your ideas and feelings.

In San Jose, California, the Latino and Asian-American population is in an uproar over a councilwoman's remarks that she insists were misunderstood, that she said were meant as compliments. Though she issued an apology, it was difficult for those who saw a videotape of her remarks to understand why she "referred to Latinos as tenacious 'pit bulls' and, using her fingers to pull her eyes into slits, said of Asians: 'If you get up and slant your eyes, you might get something out of the deal.'"[5]

The second gift is your behavior. If your conduct contradicts the vision of the community, your relationship to that community will be artificial. Your behavior must back up the common beliefs of the group. If you are part of an ethnically diverse community and yet tell racial jokes, your behavior will divide the community.

The third gift is your time. A community cannot continue to function as a community without the presence of its members. The commitment of time is a measure of how much you value the community.

The fourth gift is your rights. You must be willing to give up having your own way. This is not a matter of compromising your values and beliefs but of giving the gift of something you have rightfully earned for the good of the group.

The fifth gift is glory. The temptation to hold on to glory can be overwhelming both for the community and individuals in the community. For the good of the group you must be willing to give up your glory.

Those commitments seal the oneness of community.

The Celebration:
Enjoyment with the Communities of Otherness

In the community of otherness a woman confirms the reality of her commitment to the feminine mission. The endurance of this confirmation is cause for celebration. It is a celebration of God's grace in renewing her to continue in her mission. It is a celebration of glory, for she was formed as the glory of man and her mission continues the shout of glory to God. It is a celebration of goodness, the endurance of goodness through the redeemed. It is a celebration of gifts, the unique gifts of a woman that make her unequaled in her ability to complete and complement creation.

Discovering Your Mission

1. What is the meaning of diversity and otherness?
2. What is the advantage of community making?
3. How are you involved with diverse people groups and why?
4. How is community making a confirmation of the feminine mission?

Further Research

Using either M. Scott Peck's book *The Different Drum: Community Making and Peace* or Raleigh Washington and Glen Kehrein's *Breaking Down Walls,* expand on the concept of community and show its relevance to the feminine mission.

NOTES

1. Mark Arax, "The Child Brides of California," *The Los Angeles Times,* 4 May 1993, A-1, A-23.
2. Maurice Friedman proposes the concept of "otherness" in *The Confirmation of Otherness* (New York: Pilgrim, 1983).
3. Ibid., 136.
4. M. Scott Peck, *The Different Drum: Community Making and Peace* (New York: Simon & Schuster, 1987), 62.
5. Jennifer Warren, "San Jose Councilwoman Stirs Racial Uproar," *The Los Angeles Times,* 27 May 1993, A-3, A-33.

STUDY GUIDE

Women in the Center: Sharing the Celebration

In the popular *Back to the Future* movies produced in the 1980s, a time machine takes a teenage boy into the past, revealing how the actions of the past affect the present and how the decisions of today will affect tomorrow.

The intriguing element of the movies is the actual visualization of those changes. The boy's father, who was intimidated by the school bully in high school and continues to be cowed by the same man as an adult, wins his initial confrontation with the bully. Flashing to the present, we see the father as confident and self-assured. A sequel to the story takes the son into the future and allows him to see the consequences of his actions in the future.

A preposterous exaggeration of fiction? Yes. However, we are drawn to the concept of knowing the past and the future.

If we only knew the secrets of peace and power for women in the future we would certainly share them. It is that desire that draws women into new age rituals such as channeling and numerology. We were created with the desire to know, to share, and to celebrate our mission.

My desire is that through reading this book you will realize that you can know these secrets and that they are revealed in the inspired Scriptures. The Bible shows us that we can change the future by our actions today empowered by commitment, communications, and the confirmation of our eternal purpose.

The Celebration of Womanhood

If you want to be in the center of life, sharing in the celebration of womanhood, you can begin by accepting yourself, accepting God's sovereignty, and accepting your mission.

Accepting Self

Take some time alone and isolate yourself from the problems of others and the problems in your own life, and ask God to show you a clear picture of yourself. With a Bible and pen, begin the exploration of your mission.

The Big Picture

First, read Psalm 139 and Revelation 21–22. Record the scriptural response and your reaction to the following questions.

Psalm 139

What does God know about you? (vv. 1–6)
The Bible says: _____

_____

_____

My response: _____

_____

_____

What does that tell you about God's knowledge?

_____

_____

_____

_____

Study Guide

Where is God when you want Him (vv. 7–12)?
The Bible says: _____

_____

My response: _____

_____

What does that tell you about God's presence?

_____

_____

What did God have to do with your physical and psychological make up (vv. 13–15)?
The Bible says: _____

_____

_____

My response: _____

_____

_____

Does He know how your actions today will affect the future? How (v.16)?

_____

_____

What was the psalmist's reaction (vv. 17–18)? _____

_____

_____

What is your reaction? _____

_____

_____

The Celebration of Womanhood

What evidence is there that the psalmist was aware of the real world (vv. 19–22? _____

_____

_____

What is the modeled response to difficulty (vv. 23–24)? ___

_____

_____

What is your response? _____

_____

_____

Revelation 21–22

These chapters take us into the future. They describe the ambiance of the city of heaven prepared for those whose names are written in the Book of Life. (See 20:11–15 for a picture of the environment for those whose names are not found in the Book of Life.)

Will you be there? Why or why not (21:27)?

_____

_____

Who will have their names written in the Book of Life and be allowed entrance into heaven (2:7; 3:11, 17, 26; 3:5, 12, 21; 7:12–17)?

_____

_____

How can we "overcome" (12:11; 3:20–21; 22:17)?

_____

_____

Study Guide

How does seeing this picture of your past and your future affect your perception of who you are?

_____

_____

The Special Picture

Now think about God's specific purpose for creating you, why He made you with your particular psychological makeup, your mind, your skin color, body type, and why He made you a woman.

Start with your physical characteristics. What do you like about yourself physically? What do you not like? Why? What advantages do your physical characteristics give you in relating to other people?

_____

_____

_____

_____

Think of the inner self, your mind and emotions, your spirit, and describe your unique characteristics.

_____

_____

What does Peter say about your inner self (1 Peter 3:1–6)?

_____

_____

Accepting yourself does not mean giving in to whatever self desires. It involves the recognition of how you were formed and accepting the responsibility for your future. Why would someone who had the insight of knowledge about the future make self-defeating choices? Do you want to be an overcomer? By accepting the sacrifice of the Lamb, Jesus, who already paid for your sin, you can begin to know and accept the real self that God made you to be. As an overcomer you will be empowered and comforted by the Holy Spirit of God in your commitments, communications, and the confirmation of your eternal purpose.

Accepting God's Sovereignty

I live in California. I was raised here and returned in 1989 after seventeen years in Michigan. Though the economy is bad, fires rage, and the earthquakes continue, my husband and I still love the state.

Not everyone feels that way. Everyday I seem to hear of another family moving out. Just yesterday I heard a woman excitedly explaining that her grandmother had called from Kansas and asked her to move back there. Her husband quit his job, and they were moving into the family home. Why? "The news about the woman who was shot while testifying in church on Halloween night was just too much for me," she exclaimed. "I'm getting out."

She was afraid. I understood. I knew fear when a fax was distributed with the warning that gangs were planning to drive on the freeways with their headlights out and shoot anyone who blinked their lights at them. It turned out to be a false rumor, but it succeeded in clutching thousands with fear.

Fear is the enemy of doing right. As women we have legitimate reasons for fear. Abuse and discrimination create fear of physical and psychological problems. Yet we know, too, that our fears are sometimes founded on what might be rather than on what is.

The key to overcoming our fears is to accept the sovereignty of God. Read Psalm 27 and Isaiah 40 and think about the following:

Psalm 27

What circumstances created fear for David (vv. 1–3)?

In what circumstances do you feel fear?

What does David say will help him overcome fear (vv. 4–6)?

What does David do with his fear (vv. 7–12)?

In verse 13, David's tone abruptly changes. Why do you think that is?

What do you think he means by "wait" in verse 14? How does this action help us to do right without fear?

Isaiah 40

Verses 1–11 are words of comfort intended for the people of Israel. As the inspired Word of God, what do they tell you about God's response to your fears?

The Celebration of Womanhood

God's comfort is significant because He is sovereign (v. 10). Think about that. Why does His sovereignty make a difference?

_____

_____

What else do you learn about the character of the Comforter in verses 12–16?

_____

_____

What should you do, and what will He do about your circumstances?

_____

_____

How do you think the sovereignty of God affects your mission?

_____

_____

Accepting Your Mission

Oprah Winfrey has told thousands about the injustices that occurred in her life, yet she continues doing good for others. Why? She would say, "We are here for a purpose."

Whether you are an Oprah fan or not, you must admit that she is a doer and, believing that she has been given a unique opportunity to help people, she tries to do just that. She is generous with her wealth and possessions and giving of herself to others. She is following what she believes is her mission.

What about you? Why are you uniquely you, and how can you determine your special mission?

Study Guide

Let's go back to the beginning and examine the feminine mission, developing specific guidelines for your individual circumstances.

To Create Communion

How can you bring wholeness, companionship, support, encouragement, fellowship, and honest interaction to your relationships? Define three relationships, and write the specific actions that support that goal.

Relationship   *Actions*

1. _____   1. _____

2. _____   2. _____

3. _____   3. _____

To Inspire Vision and Hope

Think of ways that you can make life more full for those around you. Can you share your accomplishments as a mentor to others? If you are talented artistically, do you inspire hope in your performance by seeking to personally touch those in your audience? Do you affirm your friends, your spouse, your family? Do you help them to be responsible and thereby help them build new hope in themselves?

List two ways in which you can inspire vision and hope.

1. _____

2. _____

To Do Right without Fear

Sometimes when we do not do right it is not a matter of doing wrong but of simply failing to do something. Perhaps we haven't even analyzed it, but subtle fears urge us to avoid doing right. Think about your fears now. Are they fears of something physical, emotional, economic, or simply the fear that your efforts will not do any good?

What are your fears? _____

_____

What is the right thing to do? _____

_____

_____

To Affirm and Sustain Life

The actions of affirming life and sustaining life are both practical and complex. Questions about birth, healthcare, physical fitness, the environment, education, and economic and social welfare all relate to this goal of our mission.

Do you have personal gifts or training in this area? In what ways can you actively use your gifts to affirm and sustain life?

_____

_____

To Reflect Glory

That brings us full circle to our discussion of 1 Peter 3. We are a reflection of God's glory, and we glorify God by developing our inner self until our lives are illuminated by the unfading beauty of a gentle and a quiet spirit.

What are you doing, and what else could you be doing, to develop your inner self?

_____

_____

Women in the center of life are celebrating the feminine mission. Like the generation of saints described in Psalm 145:4–7, they extol the name of God.

> One generation will commend your works to another; they will tell of your mighty acts. They will speak of the glorious splendor of your majesty, and I will meditate on your wonderful works. They will tell of the power of your awesome works, and I will proclaim your great deeds. They will celebrate your abundant goodness and joyfully sing of your righteousness.

They will share the celebration.

Moody Press, a ministry of Moody Bible Institute,
is designed for education, evangelization, and edification.
If we may assist you in knowing more about Christ
and the Christian life, please write us without obligation:
Moody Press, c/o MLM, Chicago, Illinois 60610.